EASY

Windows™
for Version 3.1

Shelley O'Hara

QUe

Screen reproductions in this book were created using Collage Plus from Inner Media, Inc., Hollis, NH.

Easy Windows is based on Windows 3.1.

Publisher: David P. Ewing

Director of Publishing: Michael Miller

Managing Editor: Corinne Walls

Marketing Manager: Ray Robinson

Composed in *ITC Garamond* and *MCPdigital*.

Trademarks

All terms mentioned in this book that are known to be trademarks or service marks have been appropriately capitalized. Que cannot attest to the accuracy of this information. Use of a term in this book should not be regarded as affecting the validity of any trademark or service mark.

Microsoft and Microsoft Windows are registered trademarks of Microsoft Corporation.

Rolodex is a registered trademark of Rolodex Corporation.

Credits

Publishing Manager
Shelley O' Hara

Product Director
Robin Drake

Production Editor
Linda Seifert

Copy Editor
Patrick Kanouse

Technical Editor
Michael Watson

Novice Reviewer
Carol Estep

Cover Designer
Jay Corpus

Cover Illustrator
Susan Kinola

Book Designer
Amy Peppler-Adams

Editorial Assistants
Jill Stanley
Michelle Williams

Production Team
Angela Bannan
Claudia Bell
Danielle Bird
Anne Dickerson
Karen Dodson
Brook Farling
Bob LaRoche
Elizabeth Lewis
Tim Montgomery
Caroline Roop
Amy L. Steed
Sue VandeWalle
Michelle Worthington
Lillian Yates

Indexer
Joy Dean Lee
Johnna VanHoose

About the Author

Shelley O'Hara is a former Publishing Manager at Que Corporation. She is the author of 17 books in the Easy series, including the bestselling *Easy WordPerfect*, *Easy Word*, and *Easy 1-2-3*. She is also the coauthor of *Real Men Use DOS*. Ms. O'Hara received her bachelors degree from the University of South Carolina and her masters degree from the University of Maryland.

Contents at a Glance

Contents

A Letter from the Author

Dear Reader:

If you are a beginning user and intimidated by computers, this book is written for you. This book is set up to make it as easy as possible to learn how to use a program such as Microsoft Windows.

First, this book explains all terms and concepts so that they are easy to understand. The book doesn't assume that you know all the buzzwords of computing.

Second, this book doesn't cover every single Microsoft Windows feature. It starts with the basics and then moves on to cover the features you'll use most often in your day-to-day work.

Third, this book includes easy-to-follow steps for each procedure. It's simple to follow along with the sample exercise or to use the steps as a review.

Fourth, you don't need to worry that you might do something wrong and ruin a document or the computer. This book points out mistakes that you might make and shows you how to avoid them. This book explains how to escape from a situation when you change your mind during a procedure.

I hope that you learn a lot from this book—enough to get started and build your confidence. Armed with that confidence, you'll be ready to use your computer as it was meant to be used—as a productivity tool.

If you have any comments or suggestions on ways to improve this book, send me a note.

Sincerely,

Shelley O'Hara

Shelley O'Hara
Que Corporation
201 West 103rd Street
Indianapolis IN 46290

The Basics

- What You Can Do with Windows

- How To Use This Book

- How To Follow an Exercise

- Important Stuff To Remember

Microsoft Windows is a graphical user interface or a GUI (pronounced "gooey") that changes the way you use your computer. When you start a computer that does not have a GUI, you usually see only a two- or three-character prompt (perhaps C:\>) and a blank screen. To copy files, use programs, or make the computer work, you must type commands. This method of using a program requires that you memorize many different commands and type them correctly when you want to use the computer. Microsoft Windows makes using a computer easier.

Microsoft Windows uses a desktop metaphor. In other words, rather than displaying a blank screen when you start, Microsoft Windows displays a desktop with windows and icons. (Icons are pictures that represent other windows or programs.) This visual approach enables you to point to what you want. Starting a program, for example, is simply a matter of pointing at what you want and clicking the mouse.

The following shows the Microsoft Windows main screen:

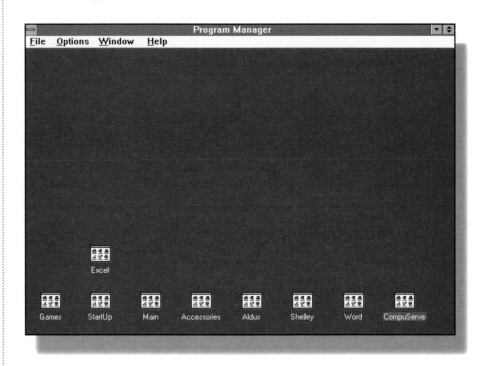

What You Can Do with Windows

With Microsoft Windows you can:

Start programs.   Rather than memorize and type commands to start a program, you point to the icon of the program that you want and double-click the mouse. The program opens on-screen in a window.

Manage files.   You can use Microsoft Windows to display files, copy files, move files, rename files, and perform other file-management tasks. You can select commands from a menu, rather than type them. You can display files in a window on-screen, and you can display several of these windows at once.

Use Microsoft Windows desk accessories.   Included with Microsoft Windows are a color paint program, a word processor, a calendar, a calculator, a notepad, a cardfile, two games, and other programs. You can use these programs to draw logos, create documents, schedule appointments, solve equations, type notes, store addresses, and have fun.

Display more than one window at a time.   When you work on a project, you don't just have one sheet of paper on your desk—you have several. One sheet might contain sales projections; one might be your current inventory list; one might be notes from sales representatives. You use all these pieces of information to create a report. Working with Microsoft Windows is the same way. You can display the information that you need in several windows and then move among the windows.

Run two programs at once.   If your computer has enough memory, you can run two programs at once and switch between them. You can enter figures in a worksheet and then pull those figures into a word-processing document.

Use Microsoft Windows-based programs.   Many programs are designed specifically to work with Microsoft Windows. These programs essentially work the same way. After you learn one Microsoft Windows program, you can learn other Microsoft Windows programs easily.

How To Use This Book

This book is set up so that you can use it several different ways:

- You can read the book from start to finish or you can start reading at any point in the book.

- You can experiment with one exercise, many exercises, or all exercises.

- You can flip through the book and look at the Before and After screens to locate specific tasks or you can look through the alphabetical task list at the beginning of the Task/Review section to find the task you want.

- You can read only the exercise, only the review, or both the Exercise and Review sections. As you learn the program, you might want to follow the exercises. After you learn the program, you can refer back to the Review section to remind yourself how to perform a certain task.

Each task includes Before and After screens that show you how the computer screen will look before and after you follow the numbered steps in the Task sections.

Task section

The Task section includes numbered steps that tell you how to accomplish certain tasks such as opening a window or starting a program. The numbered steps walk you through a specific example so that you can learn the task by doing it. The text below the numbered steps explains the concept further.

Start a program

Before

Oops! notes

You may find that you performed a task that you do not want after all. The Oops! notes tell you how to undo each procedure. In addition, the Oops! notes also may explain how to get out of a situation. By showing you how to reverse nearly every procedure, these notes allow you to use Microsoft Windows more confidently.

Oops!

If the program doesn't start, you may not have clicked twice. Point to the icon again and press the mouse button twice in rapid succession.

1 Close all group windows so that only the program group icons are displayed.
You do not have to follow this step, but doing so enables you to find the group icon that you need easily. For help with this step, see *TASK: Close a window*.

2 Double-click the Games group icon.
This step opens the Games program window. (The Before screen shows this step.) The Microsoft Windows package includes two games. The Before screen shows some additional games.

3 Double-click the Solitaire icon.
This step starts the Solitaire program. You see the cards on-screen.

For information on playing Solitaire, see your Microsoft Windows manual or *Using Windows 3.1*, Special Edition.

52   *Applications*

After you learn a procedure by following a specific example, you can refer to the Review section for a quick summary of the task. The Review section gives you the more generic steps for completing a task so that you can apply those steps to your own work. You can use these steps as a quick reference to refresh your memory about how to perform procedures.

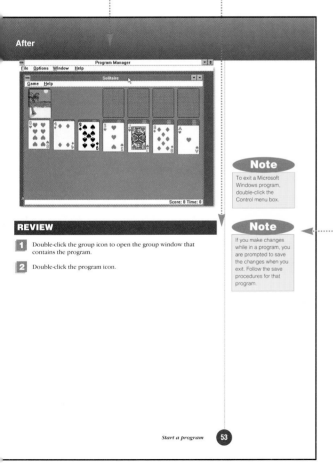

After

Note

To exit a Microsoft Windows program, double-click the Control menu box.

Note

If you make changes while in a program, you are prompted to save the changes when you exit. Follow the save procedures for that program.

Other notes

Each task contains other short notes that tell you a little more about each procedure. These notes define terms, explain other options, refer you to other sections when applicable, and so on.

REVIEW

1. Double-click the group icon to open the group window that contains the program.

2. Double-click the program icon.

Start a program **53**

How To Follow an Exercise

Microsoft Windows is flexible because it enables you to perform a task many different ways. For consistency, this book makes certain assumptions about how your computer is set up and how you use Microsoft Windows. As you follow along with each exercise, keep the following key points in mind:

- This book assumes that you followed the basic installation. It also assumes that you have installed a printer and that you have not changed any defaults.

- This book assumes that you use the mouse to select menu commands. Keyboard shortcuts are pointed out. For more information on using the keyboard, see the Reference guide in the back of this book.

- This book is based on version 3.1 of Microsoft Windows.

- Only the Before and After screens are illustrated. Screens are not shown for every step within an exercise.

Important Stuff To Remember

Now that you know the key to the book, there are just a few other things you should keep in mind. The information covered in the following sections pertains to the basics of using Microsoft Windows—the do-it-all-the-time kind of things. Take a quick look through this section before you get started.

Using a Mouse

Using the mouse is the easiest and most natural way to learn Microsoft Windows and Microsoft Windows programs. This book assumes that you are using a mouse. (Using the keyboard is covered in the "Guide to Basic Keyboard Operations" in the Reference section.)

When you move the mouse on the desk, the mouse pointer moves on-screen. You can use the mouse to

- Open windows

- Close windows

- Open menus

- Select menu commands

There are four types of mouse actions:

Action	Procedure
Point	Position the mouse pointer on an item.
Click	Position the mouse pointer on an item, press the left mouse button, and then release the mouse button.
Double-click	Position the mouse pointer on an item and press the left mouse button twice in rapid succession.
Drag	Position the mouse pointer on an item. Press and hold the left mouse button and then move the mouse. When you are finished dragging, release the mouse button.

Keep these terms in mind as you follow a task.

If you double-click the mouse and nothing happens, you might not have clicked quickly enough. Try again.

What Is the Program Manager?

The Program Manager is the central Microsoft Windows program. When you start Microsoft Windows, the Program Manager starts automatically. When you exit Microsoft Windows, you exit the Program Manager. You cannot run Microsoft Windows if you are not running the Program Manager. The Program Manager does what its name implies—it manages programs. You use it to organize applications into groups and to start programs.

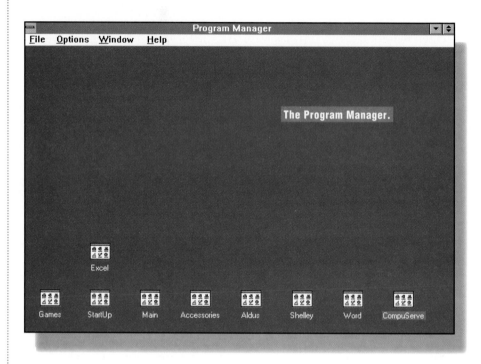

Program Groups and Icons

All programs are stored in a program group. The program group is represented by an icon. When you double-click the icon, a window is opened that displays the program icons in that group.

Program icons

Programs are also represented by icons. When you double-click a program icon, the program is started.

Windows sets up some program groups automatically:

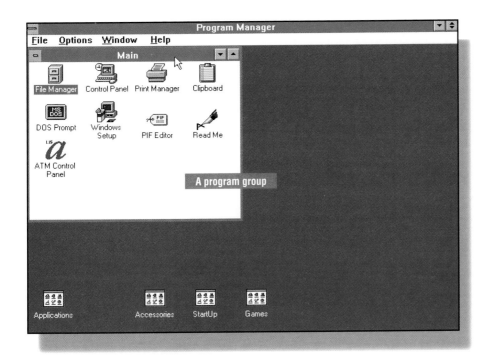

Main Program Group. The Main Program Group is created by Microsoft Windows. Within this group, you find Microsoft Windows system applications, which are programs that help you work with your system (computer). The Main Program Group includes the File Manager, Print Manager, DOS Prompt, Windows Setup, Control Panel, Clipboard, and others.

Accessories Program Group. The Accessories program group is created by Microsoft Windows and contains accessory programs that are provided with Microsoft Windows. The following list includes some of these programs:

Program	Function
Calculator	Displays a calculator on-screen.
Clock	Displays the time on-screen.
Notepad	Enables you to enter, print, and edit notes.
Calendar	Enables you to enter and review appointments.
Cardfile	Enables you to enter, edit, sort, and delete cards, similar to a Rolodex card file.
Write	Enables you to create, edit, format, and print word processing documents.
Paintbrush	Enables you to create, edit, and print drawings. Paintbrush is a complete drawing program.

Depending on how your system is set up, you may have different groups. For instance, sometimes when you purchase a new computer, the dealer will set up and install Windows and other programs. You may see different sets of program groups.

Note

Games Program Group. The Games program group contains two games: Solitaire and Minesweeper.

Startup Group. Any applications you place in the Startup group will be started when you start Windows. This group may not contain any icons.

Applications Group. When you install Microsoft Windows, the Setup program looks at the programs on your hard disk. If you have any programs that Microsoft Windows recognizes, Setup creates a program icon for them and stores them in a group named Windows Applications. It also creates a group for Non-Windows Applications.

Types of Windows

Everything in Windows is displayed in a window. There are different types of windows:

- A *program group window* displays the program icons stored in that particular program group.

- An *application window* displays the program screen. Within that area, you might see separate document windows.

- A *document window* is inside a program window. It contains the data that you type.

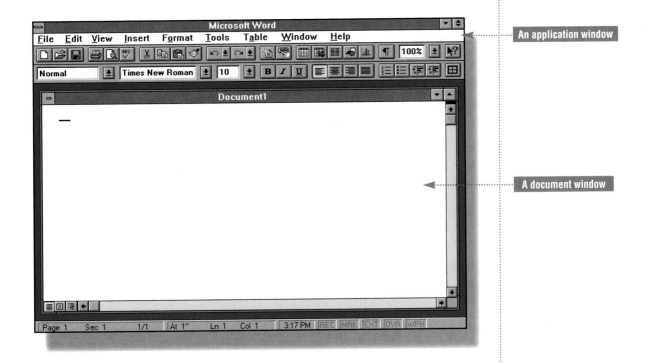

An application window

A document window

All windows have the same set of controls that enable you to move, resize, and tinker with the window. The Task section covers common window tasks.

Understanding the Windows Desktop

After you start Microsoft Windows, you see the desktop. (If you want to start the program and follow along, see *TASK: Start Microsoft Windows*. This is the first task in the Task/Review section.)

To use Microsoft Windows effectively, you should learn the different parts of the screen.

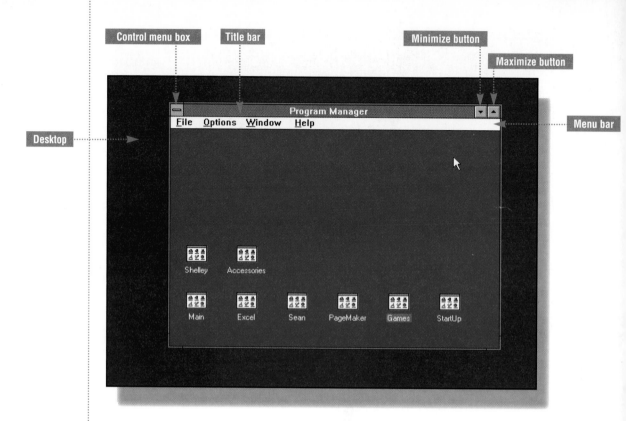

Control menu box   Title bar   Minimize button

Maximize button

Desktop

Program Manager

File   Options   Window   Help

Menu bar

Shelley   Accessories

Main   Excel   Sean   PageMaker   Games   StartUp

Note

When you work with many different windows, your desktop can become confusing. Remember that Microsoft Windows is supposed to simplify your work. To keep things simple, you can rearrange your desktop. The next time you start Microsoft Windows, it remembers this arrangement and displays the same layout on-screen.

- The desktop is the screen area on which windows and icons are displayed.

- The title bar displays the name of the window.

- The menu bar displays the Microsoft Windows menus.

- The Control menu box enables you to manipulate windows.

- The Maximize and Minimize buttons enable you to size windows.

Task/Review

- Getting Started

- Applications

- Managing Files

- Using Windows Write

- Using Paintbrush

- Customizing Windows

- Accessory Applications

Getting Started

This section covers the following tasks:

- Start Microsoft Windows

- Exit Microsoft Windows

- Get help

- Open a window

- Close a window

- Select a window

- Maximize a window

- Restore a window

- Minimize a window

- Move a window

- Resize a window

- Arrange windows

- Move an icon

- Arrange icons

Start Microsoft Windows

C:\>

The DOS prompt.

Oops!

To exit Microsoft Windows, see *TASK: Exit Microsoft Windows*.

1 **Turn on the computer and monitor.**
Every computer has a different location for its On/Off switch. Check the side, the front, and the back of your computer. Your monitor also may have a separate On switch; if so, you also need to turn on the monitor.

2 **If necessary, respond to the prompts for date and time.**
When you first turn on the computer, some systems ask you to enter the current date and time. (Many of the newer models enter the time and date automatically. If you are not prompted for these entries, don't worry.)

If you are prompted, type the current date and press Enter. Then type the current time and press Enter. Your computer keeps track of the date and time when you save files to disk. Therefore, entering the date and time ensures that your file information is complete.

3 **Type win.**
Win is the command that starts the program.

4 **Press Enter.**
Pressing Enter confirms that you want to start Microsoft Windows. The Program Manager appears in a window on-screen. The Program Manager is an application that comes with Microsoft Windows.

The Program Manager window includes many different elements, such as the menu bar, title bar, icons, and so on. See the Basics section for a description of each of these elements.

After

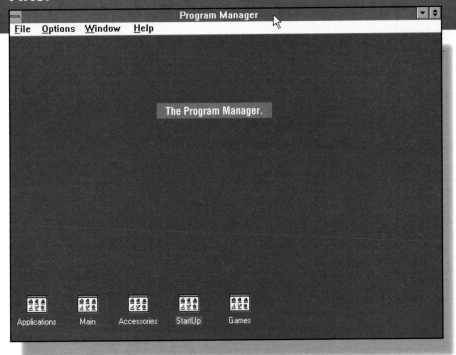

The Program Manager.

REVIEW

1 Turn on your computer and monitor.

2 Respond to the prompts for date and time, if necessary.

3 Type **win** and press **Enter.**

> **Note**
>
> An icon is a picture that represents a group window, an application, a document, or other elements within Microsoft Windows.

> **Note**
>
> A window is a rectangular area on-screen in which you view an application or a document icon.

> **Note**
>
> Some computers are set up so that when you turn them on, Windows starts automatically.

Exit Microsoft Windows

Program Manager

File   Options   Window   Help

New...
Open   Enter
Move...   F7
Copy...   F8
Delete   Del
Properties... Alt+Enter

Run...

Exit Windows...   ◄········ Click the Exit Windows command.

Applications   Main   Accessories   StartUp   Games

Oops!

If you do not want to quit, click Cancel in the Exit Windows dialog box. To restart Microsoft Windows, see *TASK: Start Microsoft Windows.*

1 **Point to File in the menu bar and click the left mouse button.**
This step opens the File menu. You see a list of File commands. The last command is Exit Windows.

2 **Point to Exit Windows and click the left mouse button.**
This step tells Microsoft Windows that you want to exit. The Exit Windows dialog box appears. This box reminds you that you are exiting the program.

3 **Point to OK and click the left mouse button.**
This step confirms that you do want to exit. You return to DOS.

```
C:\>
```

You are returned to the DOS prompt.

SHORTCUT

As a shortcut for steps 1 and 2, double-click the Control menu box.

Note

You should exit Windows before you turn off your computer.

REVIEW

1   Click **File** in the menu bar.

2   Click the **Exit** command.

3   Click **OK** or press **Enter**.

Get help

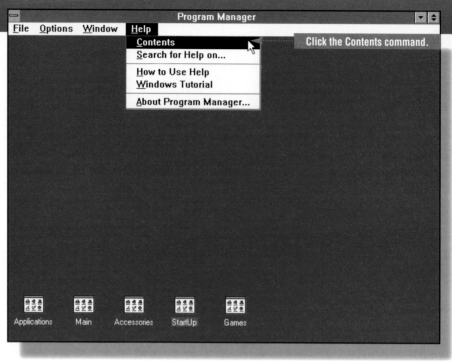

Program Manager

File   Options   Window   Help

Contents
Search for Help on...

How to Use Help
Windows Tutorial

About Program Manager...

Click the Contents command.

Applications   Main   Accessories   StartUp   Games

Oops!

To close the Help
window, point to the
Control menu box and
double-click the
mouse button.

---

1 **Point to Help in the menu bar and click the left mouse button.**
This step opens the Help menu. On-screen, you see a list of Help
menu options.

2 **Point to Contents and click the left mouse button.**
This step selects the Contents command. The Help window for the
Program Manager opens. You see the name of the Help window in
the title bar.

The Help window groups topics into these categories: How To and
Commands.

Microsoft Windows offers many ways to get Help, and the Help
feature has its own menu system. For complete information on all
Help options, see your Microsoft Windows manual or Que's *Using
Windows 3.1*, Special Edition.

3 **Point to Arrange Windows and click the left mouse button.**
This step selects the topic Arrange Windows and Icons and displays
an explanation of how to arrange windows and icons. When the
mouse pointer is on a topic for which you can get help, it changes
to a hand with a pointing finger.

4 **Point to the Control menu box and click the left mouse
button.**
The Control menu box is the small bar to the left of the window's
title bar. Clicking on this menu box displays the Control menu.

After

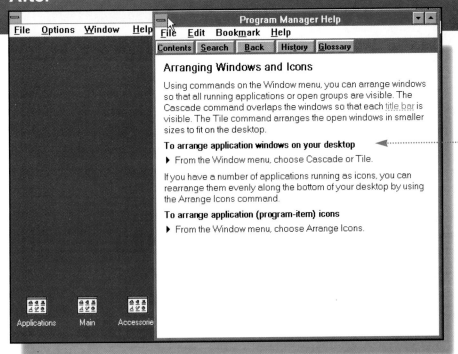

Help on arranging windows.

Note

To scroll through the Help screen, click the scroll arrow on the right side of the screen.

5 **Point to Close and click the left mouse button.**
This step selects the Close command, which closes the Help window.

REVIEW

1 Click **Help** in the menu bar.

2 Click the **Contents** command.

3 Click the topic that you want.

4 Click the **Control menu box** when you want to close the Help window.

5 Click **Close**.

SHORTCUT

As a shortcut for steps 1 and 2, press the F1 key.

Open a window

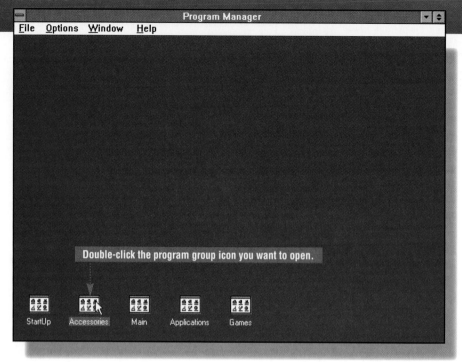

Double-click the program group icon you want to open.

StartUp   Accessories   Main   Applications   Games

Oops!

To close the window, see *TASK: Close a window*.

1 **Point to the Accessories icon.**

All programs are stored in program groups. A program group is indicated by a group icon. The name of the group appears under the group icon.

2 **Double-click the icon.**

To double-click, press the mouse button twice in rapid succession. The Accessories window appears. You see various accessory programs, such as Calculator, Calendar, and so on. These programs are provided with Microsoft Windows and are described later in this book.

After

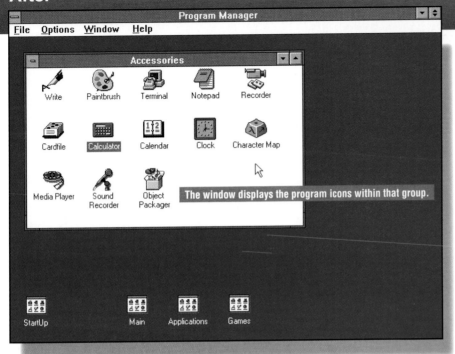

Program Manager

File   Options   Window   Help

Accessories

Write   Paintbrush   Terminal   Notepad   Recorder

Cardfile   Calculator   Calendar   Clock   Character Map

Media Player   Sound Recorder   Object Packager

The window displays the program icons within that group.

StartUp   Main   Applications   Games

REVIEW

1 Point to the group icon.

2 Double-click the mouse button.

Note

Do not worry if your screen is different from the After screen. Your desktop may be organized differently. You still can perform all the tasks.

Note

You can also use the Control menu to open a window. Click once on the Control menu box. Then click Restore.

Close a window

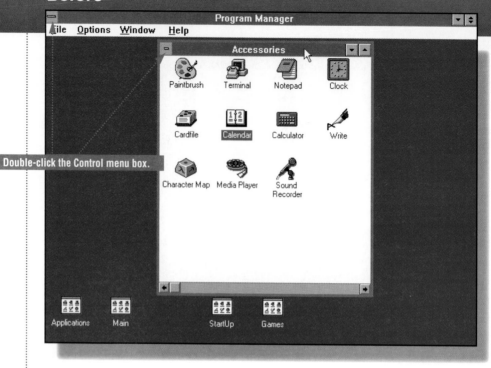

Double-click the Control menu box.

If the Exit Windows dialog box appears, you clicked on the Control menu box for the Program Manager and not for the window you want to close. Click Cancel.

1 **Open the Accessories window.**

To open the window, point to the Accessories icon and double-click the left mouse button. (Double-click means to press the mouse button twice in rapid succession.) For more information, see *TASK: Open a window*.

2 **Double-click the Control menu box.**

The Control menu box is the small bar to the left of the window's title bar. Double-clicking on this box closes the window and restores it to an icon.

Your desktop can get confusing with different windows open in different sizes. Try closing all windows and then opening just those that you need.

After

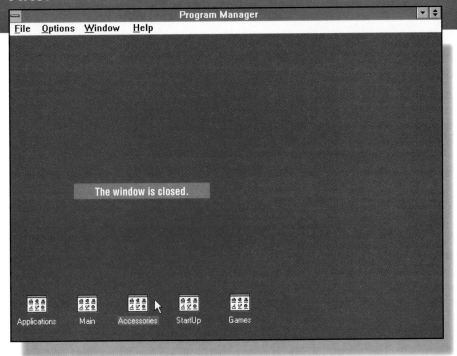

The window is closed.

Applications Main Accessories StartUp Games

REVIEW

Double-click the **Control menu box.**

Note

You can also use the Control menu to close a window. Click once on the Control menu box. Then click Close.

Select a window

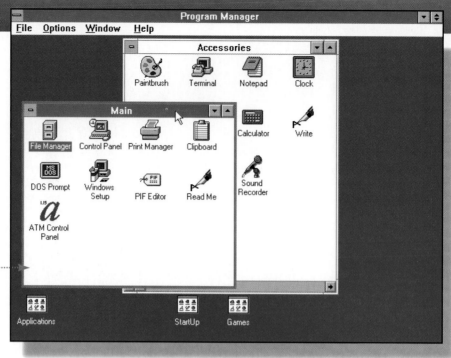

The currently active window.

Oops!

To change back to the window that was active, follow this same procedure.

1 **Open the Accessories window.**
To open the window, point to the Accessories icon and double-click the left mouse button. For more information, see *TASK: Open a window*.

2 **Open the Main window.**
To open this window, point to the Main icon and double-click the left mouse button. For more information, see *TASK: Open a window*.

You now have two windows open on-screen. The window that you just opened is the current or active window. Notice that the border and title bar of the active window are colored or shaded differently from those of the other open windows. (The title bar is the top line of the window and includes the name of the window. The border is the edge of the window.)

3 **Point to Window in the menu bar and click the left mouse button.**
This step opens the Windows menu. You see a list of numbered windows. The current window (Main) has a check mark next to it.

4 **Point to the Accessories window name and click the left mouse button.**
This step selects the Accessories window. This window moves to the top of the desktop and is the active window. The border and title bar appear in a different color or shade.

After

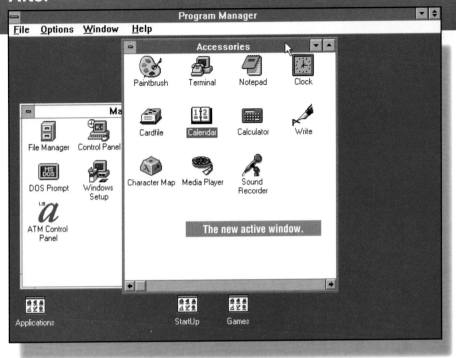

The new active window.

Note

Use this procedure to switch among windows in the Program Manager. To switch among programs, see *TASK: Switch to a different program.*

REVIEW

1 Click **Window** in the menu bar.

2 From the list, click the name of the window that you want to make active.

SHORTCUT

If you can see the window that you want on-screen, you can click anywhere on that window to select it.

Maximize a window

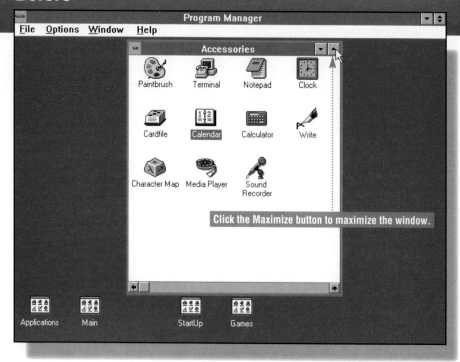

Click the Maximize button to maximize the window.

Oops!

If the Program Manager window expands, but the Accessories window doesn't, you clicked on the Maximize button for the Program Manager. Be sure to click the icons in the window you want to change.

1 **Open the Accessories window.**
To open the window, point to the Accessories icon and double-click the left mouse button. For more information, see *TASK: Open a window*.

2 **Click the Maximize button.**
The Maximize button is an up arrow in the title bar of the window. The window fills the Program Manager screen. You see Program Manager (Accessories) in the title bar.

Maximize, Minimize, and Restore are three separate functions. Maximize expands the window so that it fills the entire screen. Minimize returns the window to an icon. Restore returns the window to its last size and location.

After

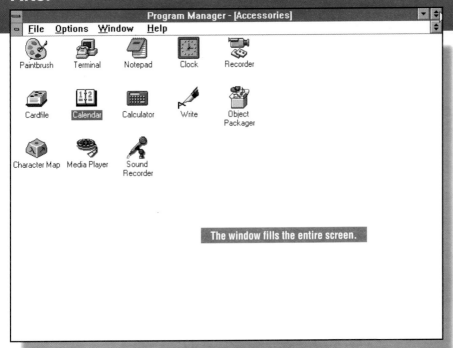

Program Manager - [Accessories]

File Options Window Help

Paintbrush Terminal Notepad Clock Recorder

Cardfile Calendar Calculator Write Object Packager

Character Map Media Player Sound Recorder

The window fills the entire screen.

REVIEW

Click the **Maximize** button.

Note

To restore the window, see *TASK: Restore a window*.

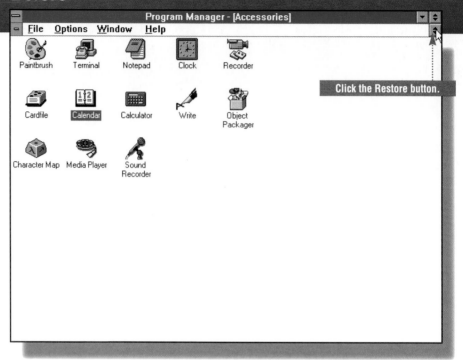

Click the Restore button.

Restore a window

Oops!

If the Program Manager window changes rather than the Accessories window, you clicked on the Restore button for the Program Manager. Try again and be sure to click the Restore button for the Accessories window.

1 **Open the Accessories window.**
To open the window, point to the Accessories icon and double-click the left mouse button. For more information, see *TASK: Open a window*.

You use Restore after you have maximized or minimized the window. For this example, you want to maximize the window.

2 **Click the Maximize button.**
This is the up arrow in the title bar of the Accessories window. This step maximizes the window. Now that the window is maximized, you can restore it to its original size.

3 **Click the Restore button.**
When you maximize a window, the Maximize button changes to a two-headed arrow, called the Restore button. Clicking this button restores the window to its original size and location.

Maximize, Minimize, and Restore are three separate functions. Maximize expands the window so that it fills the entire screen. Minimize returns the window to an icon. Restore returns the window to its last size and location.

After

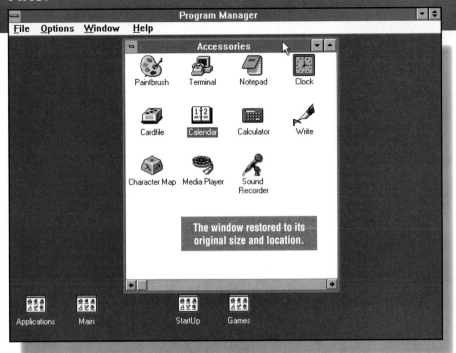

The window restored to its original size and location.

Note

You cannot restore a window unless it has been maximized or minimized.

REVIEW

1 Maximize or minimize the window.

2 Click the **Restore** button.

Note

You can also use the Control menu to restore a window. Click once on the Control menu box. Then click Restore.

Minimize a window

Program Manager

File   Options   Window   Help

Accessories

Paintbrush   Terminal   Notepad   Clock

Cardfile   Calendar   Calculator   Write

Character Map   Media Player   Sound Recorder

Click the Minimize button.

Applications   Main   StartUp   Games

Oops!

If the Program Manager window changes rather than the Accessories window, you clicked the Minimize button for the Program Manager. Try again and be sure to click the Minimize button for the Accessories window.

1 **Open the Accessories window.**

To open the window, point to the Accessories icon and double-click the left mouse button. For more information on this step, see *TASK: Open a window*.

2 **Click the Minimize button.**

The Minimize button is a down arrow in the title bar. The window is restored to an icon.

Maximize, Minimize, and Restore are three separate functions. Maximize expands the window so that it fills the entire screen. Minimize returns the window to an icon. Restore returns the window to its last size and location.

After

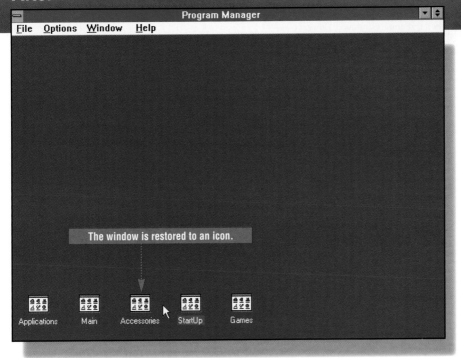

The window is restored to an icon.

Applications Main Accessories StartUp Games

REVIEW

Click the **Minimize** button.

Note

To restore the window, see *TASK: Restore a window*.

Move a window

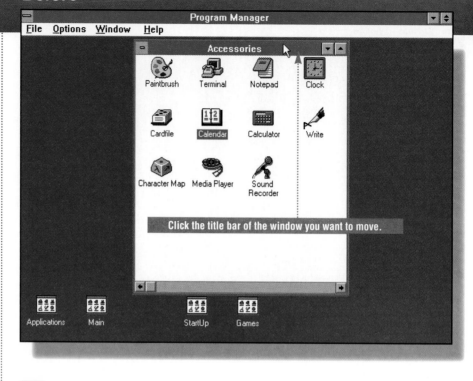

Oops!

If the window does not move, you may not have placed the mouse pointer on the title bar of the window. Reposition the mouse pointer correctly and try again.

1 **Open the Accessories window.**
To open the window, point to the Accessories icon and double-click the left mouse button. For more information, see *TASK: Open a window*.

2 **Point to the title bar.**
This step selects the window that you want to move. Be sure that you point to the title bar and not to the window border. The title bar displays the window name. Pointing to the window border resizes the window rather than moves it.

3 **Press and hold the mouse button.**
This step prepares the window to be moved. Notice that the border turns a lighter shade.

4 **Drag the mouse up and to the right until the window is in the upper right corner.**
Dragging the mouse lets you reposition the window. As you drag, you see the outline of the window.

5 **Release the mouse button.**
Releasing the mouse button moves the window to the new location.

If you have a lot of open windows and want to see them all, use the Tile command. This command automatically sizes and moves windows so that all are displayed. See *TASK: Arrange windows*.

After

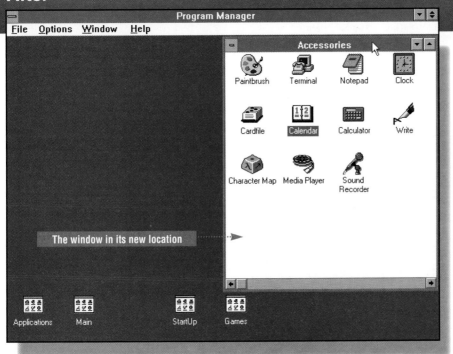

The window in its new location

REVIEW

1 Open the window that you want to move. If the window is open, select the window. See *TASK: Open a window* and *TASK: Select a window*.

2 Point to the title bar.

3 Press and hold the mouse button and drag the window to the new location.

4 Release the mouse button.

Note

If you exit the program with windows open, Microsoft Windows remembers the size and location of any open windows.

Resize a window

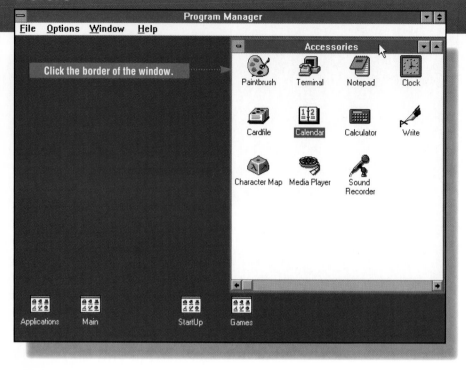

Oops!

If the window does not change, you may not have placed the mouse pointer on the border of the window. Reposition the mouse pointer correctly and try again.

1 Open the Accessories window.
To open the window, point to the Accessories icon and double-click the left mouse button. For more information, see *TASK: Open a window*.

2 Point to the left border.
This step selects the window that you want to resize. Be sure that you point to the border. When the mouse pointer is in the proper spot, it should change to a two-headed arrow.

3 Press and hold the mouse button.
This step prepares the window to be resized. Notice that the border turns a lighter shade.

4 Drag the mouse to the left until the window is about twice the size it is now.
Dragging the mouse lets you resize the window. As you drag, you see the outline of the window.

5 Release the mouse button.
Releasing the mouse button resizes the window.

After

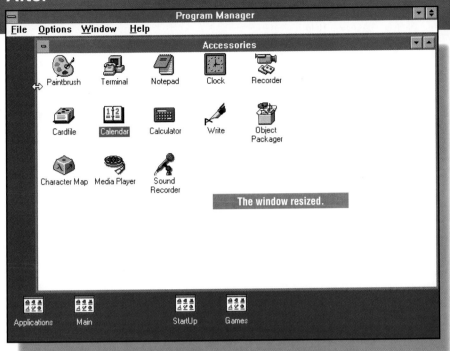

The window resized.

REVIEW

1 Open the window that you want to move. If the window is open, select the window. See *TASK: Open a window* and *TASK: Select a window*.

2 Point to one of the borders.

3 Press and hold the mouse button and drag the window to resize.

4 Release the mouse button.

Note

If you want to change both the width and the height of the window, click in the corner and then drag. Doing this enables you to resize both dimensions.

Arrange windows

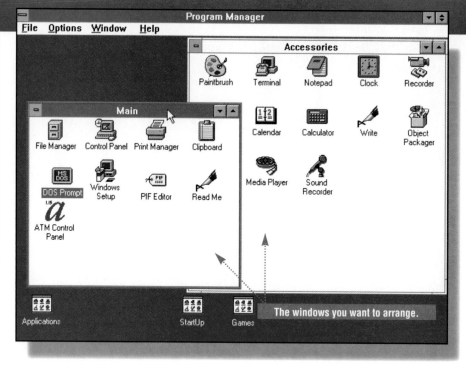

Before

(Program Manager window)

Program Manager

File   Options   Window   Help

Accessories

Paintbrush   Terminal   Notepad   Clock   Recorder

Calendar   Calculator   Write   Object Packager

Media Player   Sound Recorder

Main

File Manager   Control Panel   Print Manager   Clipboard

DOS Prompt   Windows Setup   PIF Editor   Read Me

ATM Control Panel

Applications   StartUp   Games   The windows you want to arrange.

Oops!

If you don't like the arrangement, move, resize, or close the windows.

1 Open the Accessories window.
To open the window, point to the Accessories icon and double-click the left mouse button. For more information, see *TASK: Open a window*.

2 Open the Main window.
To open this window, point to the Main icon and double-click the left mouse button.

You now have two windows open on-screen. The window that you just opened is the current or active window. Notice that the border and title bar of the active window are colored or shaded differently from the other open window.

3 Point to the Window menu and click the left mouse button.
This step opens the Windows menu.

4 Point to Tile and click the left mouse button.
This step selects the Tile command. The windows appear on-screen side by side. The icons appear at the bottom.

If you have more than two windows, the windows are arranged so that you see them all.

After

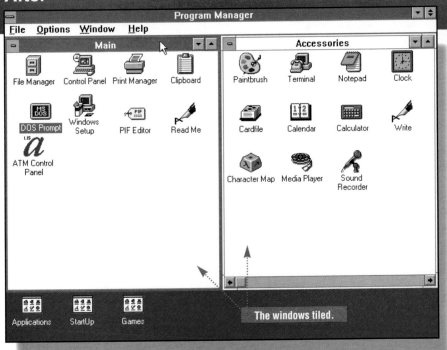

The windows tiled.

REVIEW

1 Open the windows that you want to arrange.

2 Click the **Window** menu.

3 Click the **Tile** command.

Move an icon

The icon you want to move.

Oops!

To return the icon to its original location, follow this same procedure. Or use the Arrange command; see *TASK: Arrange icons.*

1 **Close all windows so that you only see the icons.**
For information on closing a window, see *TASK: Close a window.*

2 **Point to the Accessories icon.**
This step selects the Accessories icon. When you start Microsoft Windows, all the icons are aligned at the bottom of the window. You can move the icons on the desktop.

3 **Press and hold the mouse button.**
This step selects the Accessories icon.

4 **Drag the Accessories icon to the upper left corner of the screen.**
This step moves the Accessories icon to its new location.

5 **Release the mouse button.**
Releasing the mouse button positions the Accessories icon in the new location.

After

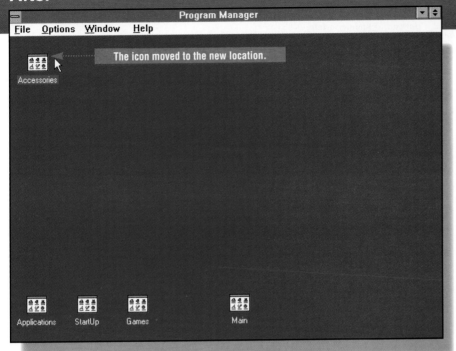

REVIEW

1 Point to the icon that you want to move.

2 Press and hold the mouse button.

3 Drag the icon to the new location.

4 Release the mouse button.

Arrange icons

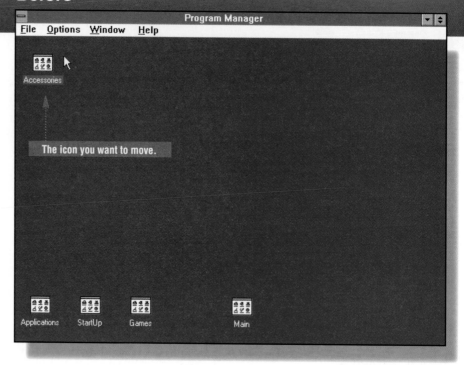

Program Manager

File   Options   Window   Help

Accessories

↑

The icon you want to move.

Applications   StartUp   Games   Main

Oops!

If you don't like the new arrangement, move the icons as you want them. See *TASK: Move an icon*.

1 **Close all windows so that you see only the group icons.**
For information on closing a window, see *TASK: Close a window*.

2 **Move the Accessories icon to the upper left corner.**
To move the icon, press and hold the mouse button and then drag the icon to the upper left corner.

For more information on moving an icon, see *TASK: Move an icon*.

3 **Point to the Window menu and click the left mouse button.**
This step opens the Window menu.

4 **Point to Arrange Icons and click the left mouse button.**
This step selects the Arrange icons command. The icons are arranged at the bottom of the window.

After

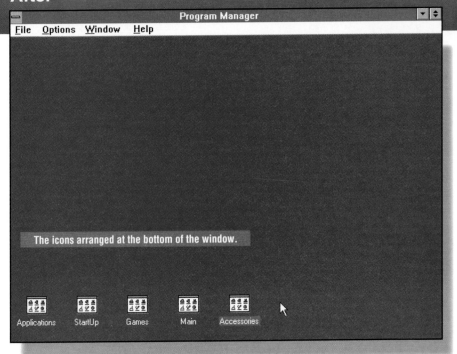

Program Manager

File   Options   Window   Help

The icons arranged at the bottom of the window.

Applications   StartUp   Games   Main   Accessories

REVIEW

1 Click the **Window** menu.

2 Click the **Arrange Icons** command.

Note

You can use this same procedure to arrange the program icons within a group window.

Applications

This section covers the following tasks:

- Start a program

- Exit a program

- Start more than one program

- Switch among programs with the Task List

- Change a program group name

- Add a new program group

- Move a program to a new group

- Copy a program icon

- Delete a program icon

- Add a new program icon

- Change a program icon

- Run a program

- Start a program automatically

- Access the DOS prompt

Start a program

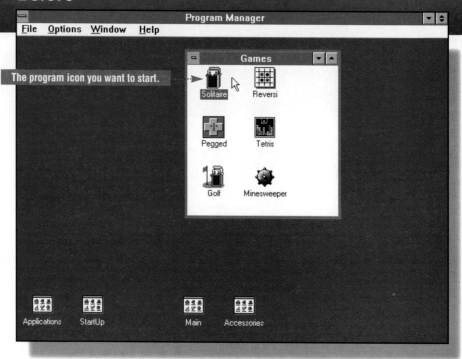

The program icon you want to start.

Oops!

If the program doesn't start, you may not have clicked twice. Point to the icon again and press the mouse button twice in rapid succession.

1 **Close all group windows so that only the program group icons are displayed.**

You do not have to follow this step, but doing so enables you to find the group icon that you need easily. For help with this step, see *TASK: Close a window*.

2 **Double-click the Games group icon.**

This step opens the Games program window. (The Before screen shows this step.) The Microsoft Windows package includes two games. The Before screen shows some additional games.

3 **Double-click the Solitaire icon.**

This step starts the Solitaire program. You see the cards on-screen.

For information on playing Solitaire, see your Microsoft Windows manual or *Using Windows 3.1,* Special Edition.

After

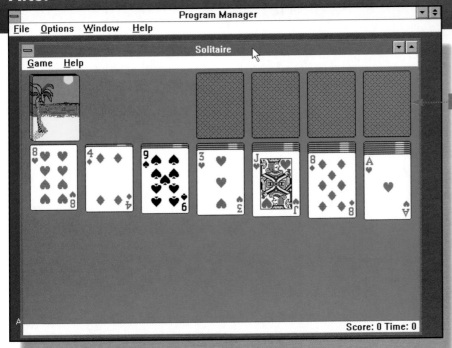

The program is started.

Note

To exit a Microsoft Windows program, double-click the Control menu box.

REVIEW

1 Double-click the group icon to open the group window that contains the program.

2 Double-click the program icon.

Note

If you make changes while in a program, you are prompted to save the changes when you exit. Follow the save procedures for that program.

Exit a program

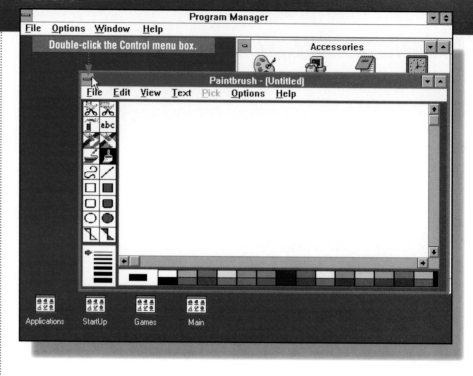

Oops!

Be sure that you save your work before you close a program. If you don't, you are reminded to save.

1 **Start the Paintbrush program.**
To do this, open the Accessories program group and double-click the Paintbrush icon. This step selects and starts the program. You see the Paintbrush draw screen.

2 **Double-click the Control menu box.**
This step closes the program. The Accessories window is still open on-screen.

After

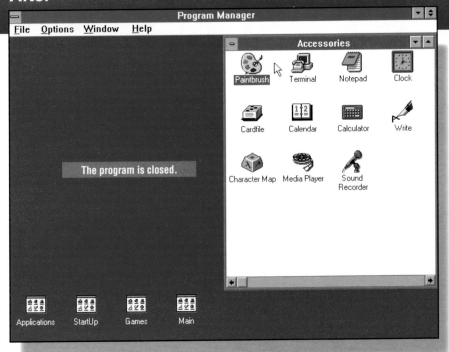

The program is closed.

REVIEW

Double-click the **Control menu box**.

Note

Exiting is different from minimizing. When you minimize a program, you restore it to an icon, but the program is still running in memory. See *TASK: Minimize a window.*

Note

Most programs have a File Exit or similar command. You can also use this command to exit a program.

Start more than one program

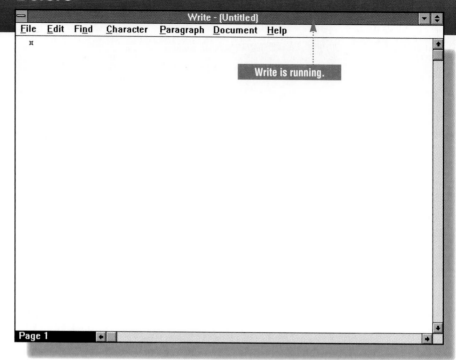

Write - [Untitled]

File Edit Find Character Paragraph Document Help

Write is running.

Page 1

Oops!

If pressing Alt+Tab doesn't display the Program Manager try using the Task List.

1 **Start the Write program.**
To do this, open the Accessories window and double-click the program icon. You see the Write program on-screen.

2 **Press Alt+Tab.**
This step returns you to the Program Manager. There are several ways to return to the Program Manager. If you can see the Program Manager window on-screen, you can click it to return to the Program Manager. Or you can use the Task List (see *TASK: Switch among programs with the Task List*).

The Accessories window should still be open.

3 **Double-click the Paintbrush icon.**
This step starts the Write program. Now both programs are running. You can switch among programs. See *TASK: Switch among programs with the Task List*.

Start the first program you want to use.

After

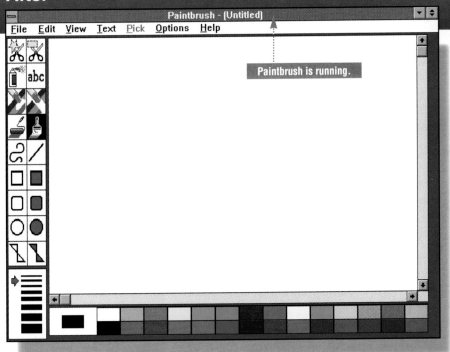

Paintbrush is running.

REVIEW

1 Start the first program you want to use.

2 Press **Alt+Tab** to return to the Program Manager.

3 Start the second program you want to use.

Note

When you exit Windows, you should exit all programs. Also, be sure you don't start the same program twice. It's easy to forget that a program is running.

Switch among programs with the Task List

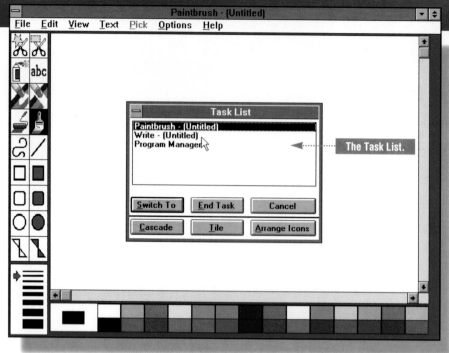

Paintbrush - [Untitled]

File   Edit   View   Text   Pick   Options   Help

Task List

Paintbrush - [Untitled]
Write - [Untitled]
Program Manager

The Task List.

Switch To   End Task   Cancel

Cascade   Tile   Arrange Icons

Oops!

To switch back to the original program, follow this same procedure.

1 Start the Write program.

To start the program, double-click the Accessories icon. Then double-click the Write icon. For help with the step, see *TASK: Run a program*.

2 Press Alt+Tab.

This step returns you to the Program Manager. There are several ways to return to the Program Manager. If you can see the Program Manager window on-screen, you can click it to return to the Program Manager. Or you can use the Task List.

3 Start the Paintbrush program.

To do this, open the Accessories window and double-click the program icon.

4 Press Ctrl+Esc.

This step displays the Task List. You see a list of the currently running programs.

5 Click Write.

This step selects the Write program.

6 Click Switch To.

This step selects the Switch To button. Now Write is the active program.

After

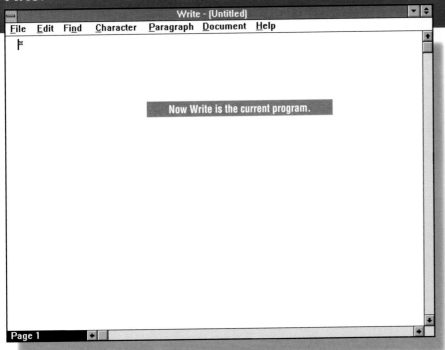

Now Write is the current program.

REVIEW

1 Press **Ctrl+Esc** to display the Task List.

2 Click the program you want.

3 Click the **Switch To** button.

Note

You can run many different Microsoft Windows programs many different ways. See your Microsoft Windows manual or *Using Windows 3.1*, Special Edition.

Change a program group name

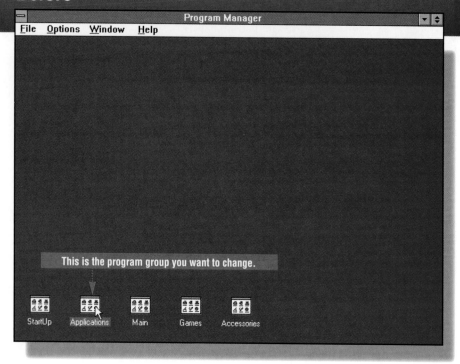

Before

Program Manager

<u>F</u>ile   <u>O</u>ptions   <u>W</u>indow   <u>H</u>elp

This is the program group you want to change.

StartUp   Applications   Main   Games   Accessories

Oops!

To change the icon names back to the original names, follow this same procedure.

1 **Point to the Applications icon and click the left mouse button.**
This step selects the Applications program group. The Control menu for this window appears.

2 **Point to File in the Program Manager menu bar and click the left mouse button.**
This steps opens the **File** menu.

3 **Point to Properties and click the left mouse button.**
This step selects the Properties command. You see the Program Group Properties dialog box. Inside this box, you see two text boxes: Description and Group File. The Description text box contains the current program group name. (The mouse pointer is positioned inside this box.)

4 **Type Microsoft Applications.**
Microsoft Applications is the new name.

5 **Press Enter.**
Pressing Enter confirms the new name. The new name appears below the icon in the Program Manager window.

60   *Applications*

After

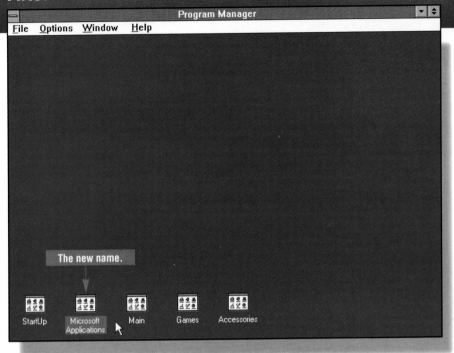

The new name.

StartUp   Microsoft   Main   Games   Accessories
Applications

REVIEW

1 Select the group icon that you want to change.

2 Click **File** in the menu bar.

3 Click the **Properties** command.

4 In the Description text box, type the new name.

5 Press **Enter**.

Note

You can create other
program groups and
move programs from
one group to another.
See *TASK: Add a new
program group* and
*TASK: Move a program
to a new group.*

Add a new program group

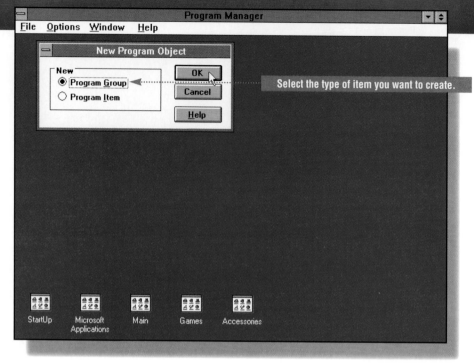

Select the type of item you want to create.

Oops!

To delete a program group, click once on the group. Then click File to open the File menu. Click the Delete command. Be careful! All the icons in the group will be deleted.

1 **Be sure all the program groups are closed.**
If a group is open and you follow the next two steps, Windows thinks you want to add a program item, rather than a group.

2 **Point to File in the menu bar and click the left mouse button.**
This step opens the File menu. You see a list of File commands.

3 **Point to New and click the left mouse button.**
This step selects the New command. You see the New Program Object dialog box. The Program Group option is selected.

4 **Click OK.**
This step confirms that you want to create a new group. You see the Program Group Properties dialog box. Inside this box, you see two text boxes: Description and Group File.

5 **Type My Stuff in the Description text box.**
This step enters a name for the new group.

6 **Click OK.**
This step confirms the new group. The group is open on-screen; no program icons appear in the group. To add icons to the group, move or copy them, as described in *TASK: Move a program to a new group* and *TASK: Copy a program icon*.

After

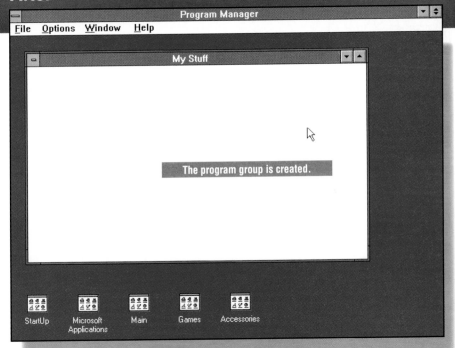

REVIEW

1 Click **File** in the menu bar.

2 Click the **New** command.

3 Click **OK**.

4 Type the name of the program group.

5 Click **OK**.

Move a program to a new group

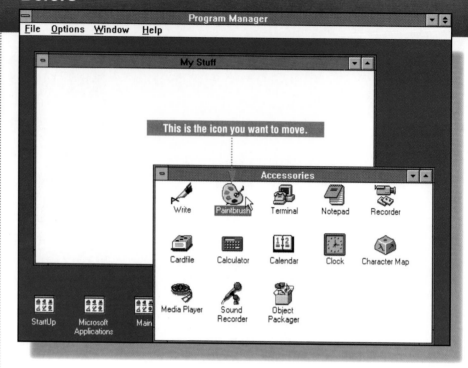

This is the icon you want to move.

Oops!

Follow this same procedure to move the icon back to the original group.

1 **Open the My Stuff and Accessories program groups.**
This step opens the groups that you want to move to and from.
To open a program group, double-click the program group icon.

2 **Arrange the windows so that you can see at least parts of both windows.**
You can either resize the windows or move them. Or you might choose to tile them. See the tasks in the Getting Started section for help on arranging open windows.

3 **Click the Paintbrush icon.**
This step selects the icon you want to move.

4 **Hold down the mouse button and drag the icon to the My Stuff group.**
This step moves the icon to the new group.

5 **Release the mouse button.**
The icon appears in the new group.

After

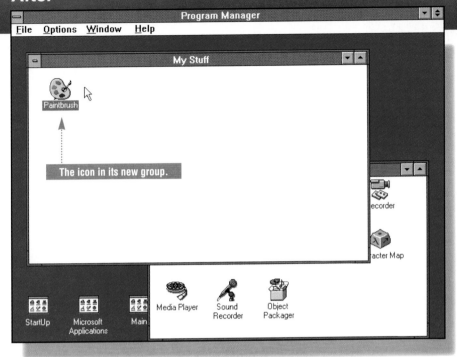

REVIEW

1 Open the window that contains the icon you want to move and the window where you want to place the icon.

2 Click the icon and drag it to the new window.

3 Release the mouse button.

Note

You cannot move an icon onto the desktop. You see the universal No sign if you try to drop the icon on the desktop.

Copy a program icon

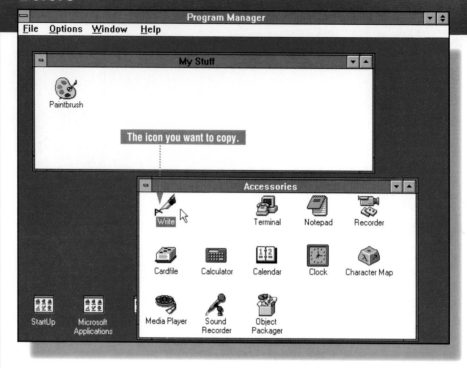

Program Manager

<u>F</u>ile <u>O</u>ptions <u>W</u>indow <u>H</u>elp

My Stuff

Paintbrush

The icon you want to copy.

Accessories

Write   Terminal   Notepad   Recorder

Cardfile   Calculator   Calendar   Clock   Character Map

Media Player   Sound Recorder   Object Packager

StartUp   Microsoft Applications

Oops!

To delete an icon, see *TASK: Delete a program icon.*

1 **Open the My Stuff and Accessories program groups.**
This step opens the groups that you want to copy to and from.
To open a program group, double-click the program group icon.

2 **Arrange the windows so that you can see at least parts of both windows.**
You can either resize the windows or move them. Or you might choose to tile them.

3 **Click the Write icon.**
This step selects the icon you want to copy.

4 **Hold down the Ctrl key.**
Holding down the Ctrl key tells Windows that you want to copy—not move—the icon.

5 **Hold down the mouse button and drag the icon to the My Stuff group.**
This step copies the icon to the new group.

6 **Release the mouse button.**
The icon appears in the new group and the original group.

After

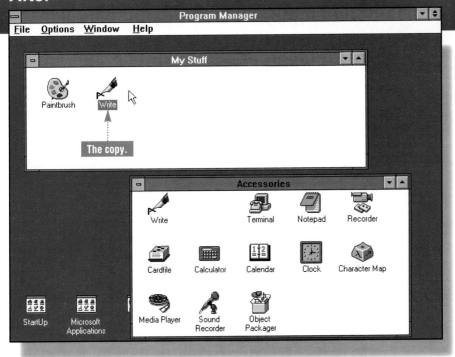

1 Open the window that contains the icon you want to copy and the window where you want to place the copy of the icon.

2 Hold down the **Ctrl** key.

3 Click the icon and drag it to the new window.

4 Release the mouse button.

Note

If several people use your computer, set up groups for each of them. Then copy or move the icons that person uses into his or her program group.

Delete a program icon

Program Manager

File   Options   Window   Help

My Stuff

Paintbrush   Write   ◄········· The icon you want to delete.

Accessories

Write   Terminal   Notepad   Recorder

Cardfile   Calculator   Calendar   Clock   Character Map

Media Player   Sound Recorder   Object Packager

StartUp   Microsoft Applications

Oops!

Click No for step 5 (task) if you change your mind. Or you can add the program icon back. See *TASK: Add a new program icon.*

1 Open the My Stuff program group.
This step opens the My Stuff program group. (This task assumes that you've created this group and copied the Write icon to it.)

2 Click the Write icon.
This step selects the icon you want to delete. In this case, the icon is a copy of an existing icon. You should be careful when deleting icons; restoring them may be difficult.

3 Click File in the menu bar.
This step opens the File menu and displays a list of File commands.

4 Click the Delete command.
You see the Delete dialog box. This dialog box asks you to confirm that you want to delete the icon.

5 Click Yes.
This step selects the Yes button. The icon is deleted.

After

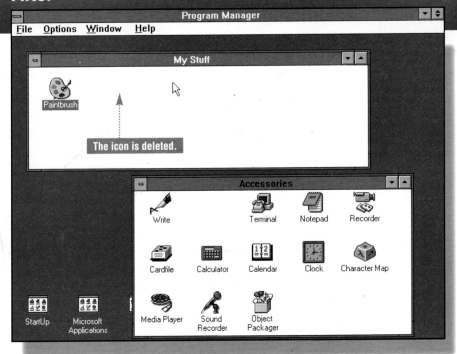

REVIEW

1 Click the icon you want to delete.

2 Click **File** in the menu bar.

3 Click the **Delete** command.

4 Click the **Yes** button.

Note

When you delete the icon, you *don't* delete the program files on disk. The files are still there. You can restore the program icon if you want.

Note

To delete a program group, click it. Then follow this same procedure. All icons in that group will also be deleted.

Add a new program icon

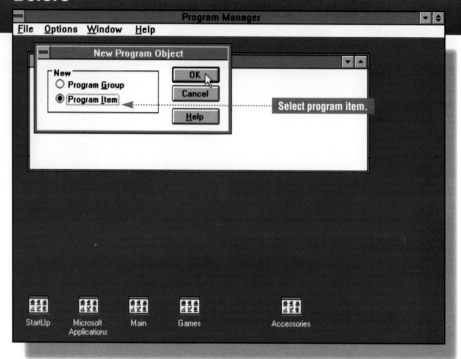

Program Manager

File   Options   Window   Help

New Program Object

─ New ─
○ Program Group
● Program Item

OK
Cancel
Help

Select program item.

StartUp   Microsoft   Main   Games   Accessories
          Applications

Oops!

See *TASK: Delete a program icon* for information on deleting a program icon.

1 **Open the My Stuff group.**
This is the group you want to add the icon to. If you don't have this group, open one you do have.

2 **Point to File in the menu bar and click the left mouse button.**
This steps opens the File menu. You see a list of File commands.

3 **Point to New and click the left mouse button.**
This step selects the New command. You see the New Program Object dialog box. The Program Item option is selected.

4 **Click OK.**
This step confirms that you want to create a new group. You see the Program Item Properties dialog box. Inside this box, you see these text boxes: Description, Command Line, Working Directory, and Shortcut Key.

5 **Type Clock in the Description text box and press Tab.**
This step enters a name for the new program and moves the insertion point to the Command Line text box. This is where you type the command to start the program. You may also need to type the directory that contains the program.

After

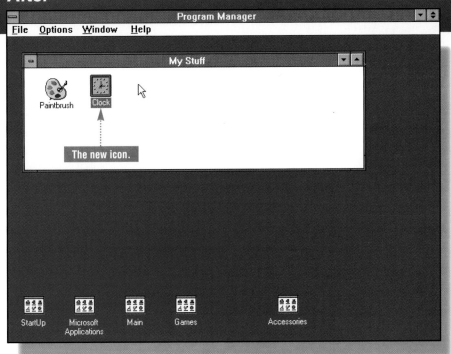

The new icon.

6 **Type C:\WINDOWS\CLOCK.EXE.**
This step enters the program name. Program names usually end in EXE, COM, or BAT. If you don't know the program name, you can browse through the directories to find it. See *Using Windows 3.1,* Special Edition for help on using the Browse button.

7 **Click OK.**
This step adds the new program.

REVIEW

1 Click **File** in the menu bar.

2 Click the **New** command.

3 Click **OK**.

4 Type the name of the program and press **Tab**.

5 Type the command to start the program.

6 Click **OK**.

Note

When you install most Windows programs, they create their own program group and icons. There may be times when you want to add a new program (maybe a DOS program). You can use this procedure.

Note

Adding a program isn't always easy. You have to know the file name and know where that file is kept on your hard disk. See *Using Windows 3.1*, Special Edition for complete information on adding new programs.

Change a program icon

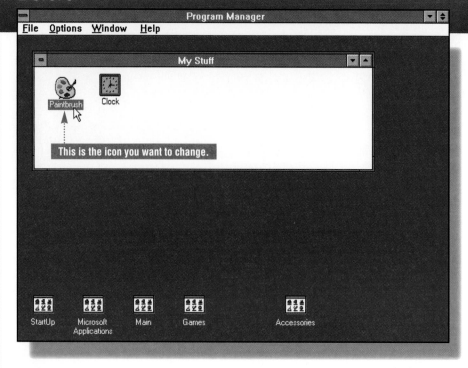

My Stuff

This is the icon you want to change.

StartUp   Microsoft   Main   Games   Accessories
Applications

Oops!

To go back to the
original icon, follow
steps 1 through 4. In
the File Name text box,
type C:\WINDOWS\
PBRUSH.EXE. Then
click OK.

1 **Point to the Paintbrush icon and click the left mouse button.**
This step selects the icon you want to change.

2 **Point to File in the menu bar and click the left mouse button.**
This steps opens the File menu.

3 **Point to Properties and click the left mouse button.**
This step selects the Properties command. You see the Program
Item Properties dialog box. Inside this box, you see the Description,
Command Line, Working Directory, and Shortcut Key for the
selected program.

4 **Click the Change Icon button.**
This step selects the Change Icon button and opens the Change
Icon dialog box. You see the current icon listed.

5 **Click the Browse button.**
This step opens the Browse dialog box. Here you are looking for
another file that contains program icons.

6 **Scroll through the list until you see the file MORICONS.DLL.
Double-click this file**.
This step selects the MORICONS file. This is a Windows file that
contains additional icons. You see the icons in a strip in the dialog
box.

After

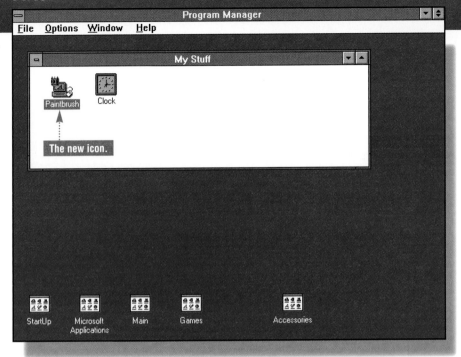

---

7 Click the scroll arrows until you see the 10th icon. Click it.
This step selects the icon you want.

8 Click OK in the Change Icon dialog box and in the Program
Item Properties dialog box.
This step closes all the dialog boxes. The new icon appears.

REVIEW

1 Select the program icon that you want to change.

2 Click **File** in the menu bar.

3 Click the **Properties** command.

4 Click the **Change Icon** button.

5 Type the name of the file that contains the icon. Or use the **Browse**
button to find the file.

6 Click the icon you want.

7 Click **OK** twice.

Before

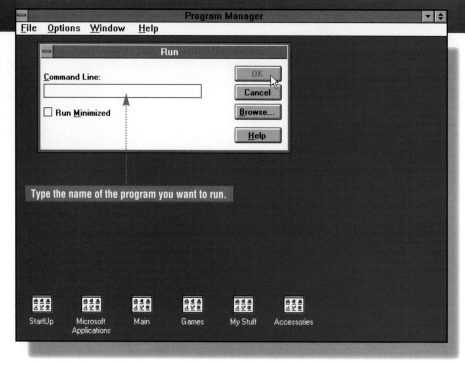

Run a program

Oops!

To exit the program, see *TASK: Exit a program*.

1 **Click File in the menu bar.**
This step opens the File menu. You see a list of File commands.

2 **Click the Run command.**
This step selects the Run command. You see the Run dialog box. Type the command to start the program in this dialog box.

3 **Type WRITE.EXE in the Run dialog box.**
This step enters the program's file name.

4 **Click OK.**
This step starts the program.

After

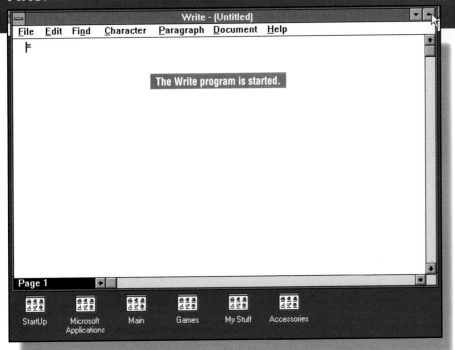

The Write program is started.

REVIEW

1 Click **File** in the menu bar.

2 Click the **Run** command.

3 Type the program file name.

4 Click **OK**.

Note

Use this procedure when you haven't created a program icon for the program. You also use File Run when you are installing a new program and running the INSTALL or SETUP program from the floppy disk.

Start a program automatically

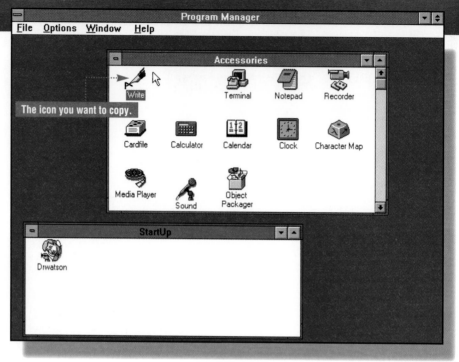

Oops!

If you don't want the program to start, delete the icon in the StartUp group. Or move the icon to another group.

1 **Open the My Stuff and StartUp program groups.**
This step opens the groups that you want to copy to and from.
To open a program group, double-click the program group icon.

2 **Arrange the windows so that you can see at least parts of both windows.**
You can either resize the windows or move them. Or you might choose to tile them. See the tasks in the Getting Started section for help on arranging open windows.

3 **Click the Write icon.**
This step selects the icon you want to copy.

4 **Hold down the Ctrl key.**
Holding down the Ctrl key tells Windows that you want to copy—not move—the icon.

5 **Hold down the mouse button and drag the icon to the StartUp group. Release the mouse button.**
This step copies the icon to the new group. The next time you start Windows, Write will start automatically.

After

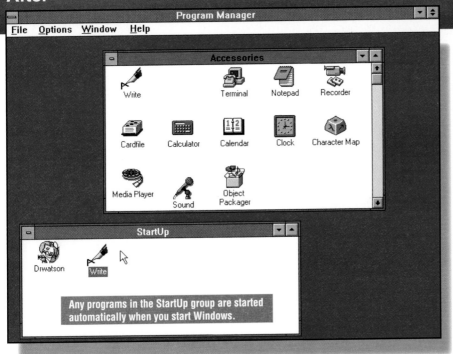

Any programs in the StartUp group are started automatically when you start Windows.

REVIEW

1 Open the window that contains the icon you want to copy and the StartUp group.

2 Hold down the **Ctrl** key.

3 Click the icon and drag it to the **StartUp** window.

4 Release the mouse button.

Access the DOS prompt

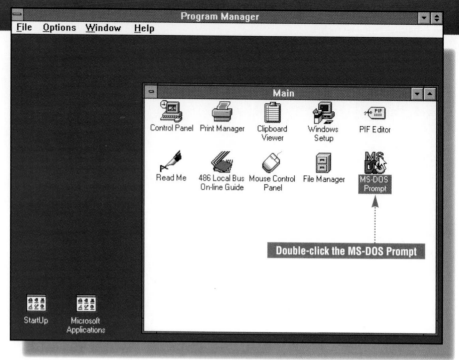

Program Manager

File Options Window Help

Main

Control Panel   Print Manager   Clipboard Viewer   Windows Setup   PIF Editor

Read Me   486 Local Bus On-line Guide   Mouse Control Panel   File Manager   MS-DOS Prompt

Double-click the MS-DOS Prompt

StartUp   Microsoft Applications

Oops!

Don't type WIN to restart Windows again. Windows is still started. Instead, type EXIT to return to the Program Manager.

1 **Open the Main program group.**
This step opens the program group that contains the MS-DOS Prompt program icon.

2 **Double-click the MS-DOS Prompt icon.**
This step temporarily exits Windows and returns you to a DOS prompt. You can type a DOS command.

3 **Type DIR and press Enter.**
You see a list of the files on-screen.

4 **Type EXIT and press Enter.**
This step returns you to Windows.

After

```
WPWIN     REG      1245 09-10-93    3:52p
WORDWIZ   INI      1710 09-22-93    4:45p
_MSSETUP  BAK       836 08-18-93    9:23a
TTEMBED   INI       280 04-23-93   12:00a
MSFNTMAP  INI       611 06-29-93   12:00a
WINHELP   INI        57 10-02-93    9:14a
WINWORD6  INI      1224 10-11-93   11:53a
MSTXTCNV  INI       355 08-18-93    9:23a
FILEMAN   INI       266 09-23-93    8:33a
FS5LPT1   PCL      4714 10-20-93   11:02a
WPCSET    WCS     28361 08-27-93    2:53p
DASHZAP   EXE     13792 06-21-93   12:00a
EXCEL5    XLB      1163 10-25-93   11:17a
MSFFILE   INI       276 10-22-93    2:45p
_FF_00    TMP     14980 09-26-93   12:13p
~XLCBHLP  TMP       226 10-11-93    3:45p
EXCEL5    INI      1392 10-25-93   11:21a
MICROSOF  GRP      1592 10-29-93    9:20a
CCMAIL        <DIR>      10-18-93    8:01a
ARTGALRY  INI        83 10-18-93    9:53a
MSWORKS3  INI      3432 10-18-93    9:54a
      349 file(s)     9006995 bytes
                     76161024 bytes free

C:\WINDOWS>
```

The results of the DIR command.

REVIEW

1 Open the **Main** program group.

2 Double-click the **MS-DOS Prompt** icon.

3 Type any DOS commands you want.

4 Type **EXIT** and press **Enter** to return to Windows.

Note

There are some DOS commands you shouldn't run from the DOS prompt. Check your DOS manual.

Managing Files

This section covers the following tasks:

- Open the File Manager
- Expand directories
- Collapse directories
- Change the File Manager view
- Select a drive
- Display files
- Sort files
- Change the file view
- Display only selected files
- Select a file
- Select multiple files
- Open two windows
- Tile the windows
- Copy a file
- Delete a file
- Rename a file
- Move a file
- Search for a file
- Create a directory
- Rename a directory
- Move a directory
- Remove a directory
- Format a diskette
- Copy a diskette
- Run a program from the File Manager
- Change the font used in File Manager
- Close the File Manager

Open the File Manager

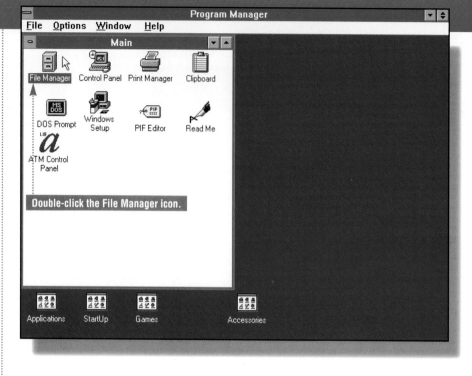

Before

Double-click the File Manager icon.

Oops!

To close the File Manager, double-click the Control menu box next to the File Manager title bar.

1 **Point to the Main group icon and double-click the mouse button.**
This step opens the Main window. Double-click means to click the mouse button twice in rapid succession. This window stores programs—including the File Manager.

You see icons for various programs: File Manager, Control Panel, Clipboard, and so on. These programs are provided with Windows.

2 **Point to the File Manager icon and double-click the mouse button.**
The File Manager icon looks like a file drawer. This step opens the File Manager window. By default, the File Manager window is not maximized. To avoid clutter, maximize the window.

3 **Click the Maximize button in the title bar.**
The Maximize button is the up arrow in the title bar. This step expands the File Manager window so that it fills the screen.

At the top of the File Manager window, you see the title bar and the menu bar. Beneath the menu bar, you see a window that displays icons for the available drives, a directory list, and a file list. The name of the current directory appears in the title bar of this window.

After

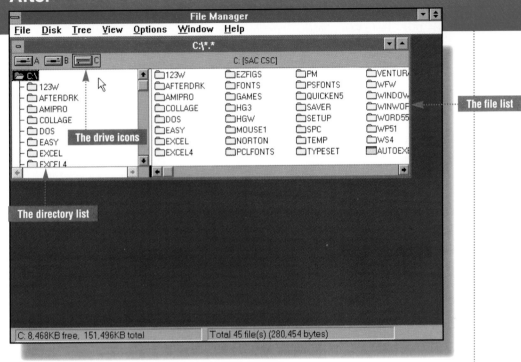

The file list

The drive icons

The directory list

The left side of the window shows the directory list and is called the Directory Tree window. Scroll arrows for this part of the window appear in the middle of the window. If the entire contents of the window are displayed, the scroll arrows are dimmed.

The directories on your hard disk are represented by folder icons. The directories appear in the list in alphabetical order.

The right side of the window is called the file list window. This part displays the files in the selected directory (the directory that is highlighted in the Directory Tree window). The scroll arrows for this window appear along the bottom of the window.

At the bottom of the File Manager window, you see the number of bytes free, total bytes, and total number of files.

Your computer screen will look different from the Before and After screens because your hard drive will have difference directories.

REVIEW

1 Double-click the **Main** group icon.

2 Double-click the **File Manager** icon.

> **Note**
>
> You can resize the file list window so that it can display more files. See *TASK: Resize a window.*

> **Note**
>
> Although the Directory Tree Window has a Control menu box, you cannot close this window. It is always open when the File Manager is open.

Expand directories

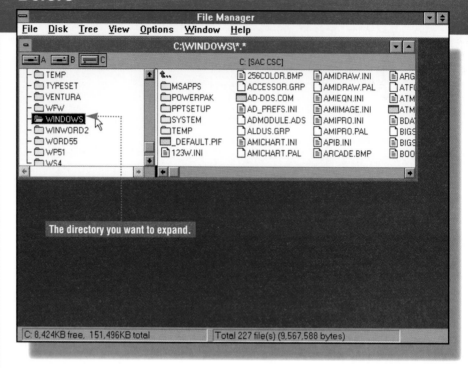

The directory you want to expand.

1 **Open the File Manager.**
To open the File Manager, double-click the Main group icon. Then double-click the File Manager icon. For more information on this step, see *TASK: Open the File Manager*.

The Directory Tree window appears on the left side. This window lists the directories in the root (or main) directory of drive C.

2 **Click the down scroll arrow until you see the directory called WINDOWS.**
This step enables you to see additional directories in the root directory of drive C. The down scroll arrow is located in the middle of the window.

The Before screen shows this step.

3 **Double-click the WINDOWS directory icon if the folder is not open already.**
This step expands the WINDOWS directory. You see the directories that are contained within this directory. You may have to scroll the window to see all the directories.

After

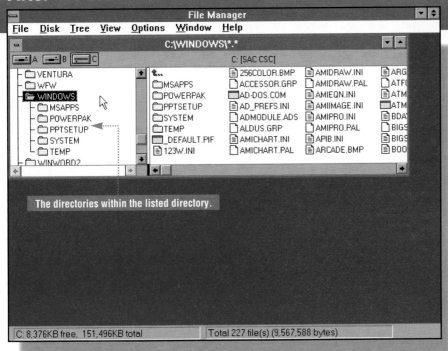

The directories within the listed directory.

REVIEW

1 Open the **File Manager**.

2 Point to the icon of the directory that you want to expand.

3 Double-click the mouse button.

Note

The root directory is the main directory. All other directories branch off from this main directory.

Note

To collapse a directory, see *TASK: Collapse directories*.

Collapse directories

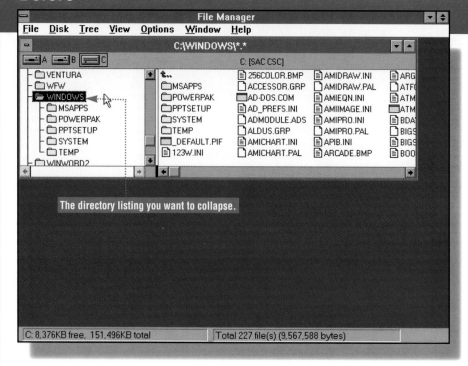

The directory listing you want to collapse.

1 **Open the File Manager.**
To open the File Manager, double-click the Main group icon. Then double-click the File Manager icon. For more information on this step, see *TASK: Open the File Manager*.

2 **Expand the WINDOWS directory.**
You may have to scroll through the window to find the WINDOWS directory. The scroll arrows appear on the right side of the window. To scroll, click the scroll arrow that points in the direction that you want to scroll. To scroll up, for example, click the up scroll arrow.

To collapse a directory, it must be expanded first. To expand the directory, double-click the directory icon. The directories within this directory appear under the WINDOWS directory name. (The Before screen shows this step.)

3 **Double-click the WINDOWS directory icon.**
This step collapses the directory. Be sure that you click the directory icon and not the directory name.

After

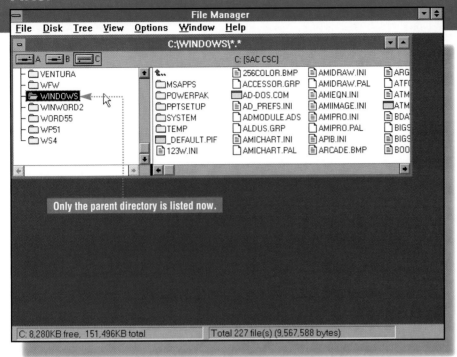

Only the parent directory is listed now.

REVIEW

1 Open the **File Manager**.

2 Point to the icon of the directory that you want to collapse. Remember that you can collapse only expanded directories.

3 Double-click the mouse button.

Change the File Manager view

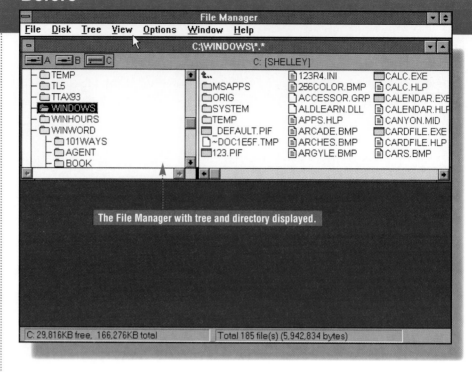

The File Manager with tree and directory displayed.

Oops!

Select the View, Tree and Directory command to return to the original view.

1 **Open the File Manager.**
To open the File Manager, double-click the Main group icon. Then double-click the File Manager icon. For more information on this step, see *TASK: Open the File Manager*.

2 **Click View in the menu bar.**
This step opens the View menu and displays a list of View commands.

3 **Click the Tree Only command.**
This step selects the Tree Only command. You now see just the list of directories (the tree) and not the directory contents. Rather than two panes, you just have one.

After

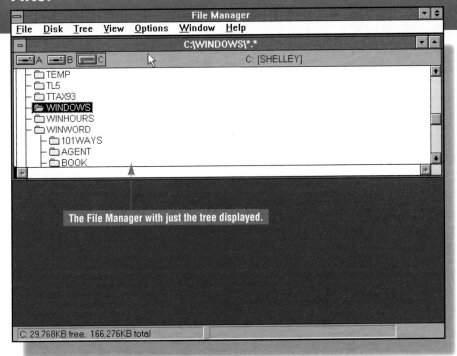

The File Manager with just the tree displayed.

REVIEW

1   Click **View** in the menu bar.

2   Click the **Tree Only** command.

Note

If you want to display just the directory contents, select Directory Only for step 3 (task section).

Select a drive

File Manager

File   Disk   Tree   View   Options   Window   Help

C:\WINDOWS*.*

A   B   C

C: [SAC CSC]

SETUP
SPC
TEMP
TYPESET
VENTURA
WFW
WINDOWS
WINWORD2
WORD55
WP51
WS4

MSAPPS
POWERPAK
PPTSETUP
SYSTEM
TEMP
_DEFAULT.PIF
123W.INI
256COLOR.BMP
ACCESSOR.GRP
AD-DOS.COM

AD_PREFS.INI
ADMODULE.ADS
ALDUS.GRP
AMICHART.INI
AMICHART.PAL
AMIDRAW.INI
AMIDRAW.PAL
AMIEQN.INI
AMIIMAGE.INI
AMIPRO.INI
AMIPRO.PAL

APIB.INI
ARCADE.BMP
ARGYLE.BMP
ATFONT.DLL
ATM.INI
ATMCNTRL.EXE
BDAY.TXT
BIGSKY.HLP
BIGSKY.INI
BOOTLOG.TXT
BOXES.BMP

BUS
BUS
CAL(
CAL(
CAL
CAL
CAN1
CAR
CAR
CAS
CHA

Click the drive icon you want.

C: 8,280KB free, 151,496KB total   Total 227 file(s) (9,567,588 bytes)

Oops!

If you see the message There is no disk in drive A:, **you didn't insert a disk into the drive or you didn't close the drive door. Insert the disk, close the door, if necessary, and click Retry.**

1 Open the File Manager.
To open the File Manager, double-click the Main group icon. Then double-click the File Manager icon. For more information on this step, see *TASK: Open the File Manager*.

2 Insert a floppy disk into floppy drive A.
You are inserting the disk that you want to use. Most computers have at least one floppy drive, which is called drive A. You also may have additional floppy drives. If you are inserting a 5 1/4-inch disk, be sure that you close the drive door after you insert the disk into the drive. If the door isn't closed, the computer cannot read the information on the disk.

3 Click the drive A icon.
This step selects drive A and displays the folders (or directories) on this drive. If the disk does not contain any directories, you only see A:\ next to a directory icon in the Directory Tree window.

After

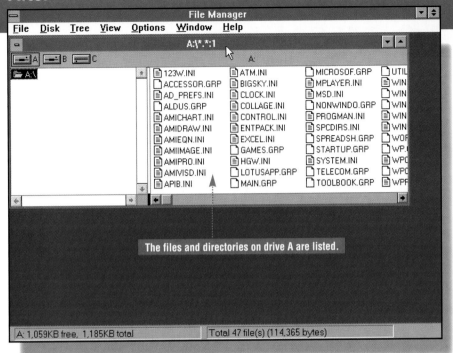

The files and directories on drive A are listed.

REVIEW

1 Open the **File Manager**.

2 Insert the floppy disk that you want to use into a drive.

3 Click the icon for that drive.

Note

To change the directory back to drive C, click the disk drive C icon.

Display files

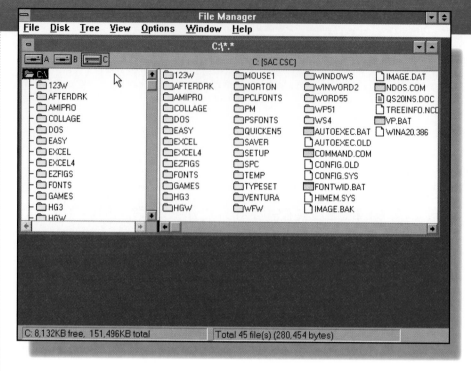

C:*.*

A   B   C   C: [SAC CSC]

C:\
├ 123W
├ AFTERDRK
├ AMIPRO
├ COLLAGE
├ DOS
├ EASY
├ EXCEL
├ EXCEL4
├ EZFIGS
├ FONTS
├ GAMES
├ HG3
├ HGW

123W	MOUSE1	WINDOWS	IMAGE.DAT
AFTERDRK	NORTON	WINWORD2	NDOS.COM
AMIPRO	PCLFONTS	WORD55	QS20INS.DOC
COLLAGE	PM	WP51	TREEINFO.NCD
DOS	PSFONTS	WS4	VP.BAT
EASY	QUICKEN5	AUTOEXEC.BAT	WINA20.386
EXCEL	SAVER	AUTOEXEC.OLD	
EXCEL4	SETUP	COMMAND.COM	
EZFIGS	SPC	CONFIG.OLD	
FONTS	TEMP	CONFIG.SYS	
GAMES	TYPESET	FONTWID.BAT	
HG3	VENTURA	HIMEM.SYS	
HGW	WFW	IMAGE.BAK	

C: 8,132KB free, 151,496KB total   Total 45 file(s) (280,454 bytes)

Oops!

To display files in a different directory, click that directory in the Directory Tree window.

1 **Open the File Manager.**
To open the File Manager, double-click the Main group icon. Then double-click the File Manager icon. For more information on this step, see *TASK: Open the File Manager*.

2 **Click the WINDOWS directory.**
The WINDOWS directory contains the files that you want to display.

You may have to scroll through the list to find WINDOWS.
The scroll arrows appear in the middle of the window.

When you click a directory, the files in that directory are listed in the file list window (on the right side of the File Manager window). The folder icon changes so that it looks like an open file.

After

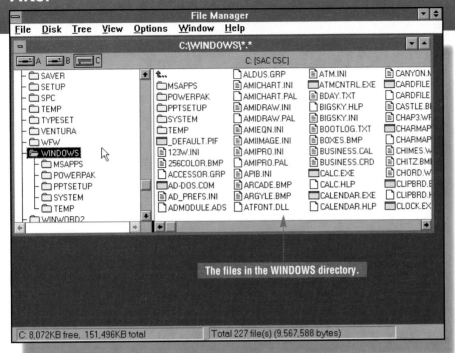

The files in the WINDOWS directory.

REVIEW

1 Open the **File Manager**.

2 Click the directory that contains the files you want to display.

Sort files

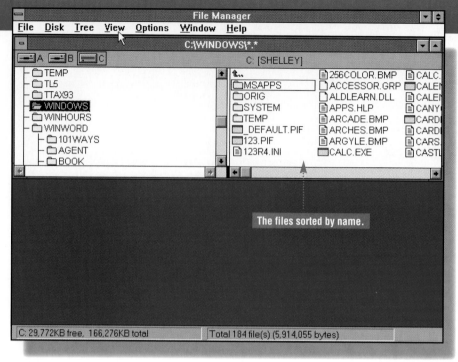

The files sorted by name.

1 **Open the File Manager.**
To open the File Manager, double-click the Main group icon. Then double-click the File Manager icon. For more information on this step, see *TASK: Open the File Manager*.

2 **Click View in the menu bar.**
This step opens the View menu and displays a list of View commands.

3 **Click the Sort by Type command.**
This step selects the Sort by Type command. The files are now listed in alphabetical order by type. (The extension indicates the type of file.)

After

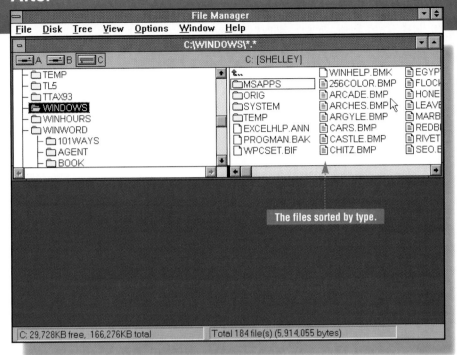

The files sorted by type.

REVIEW

1 Click **View** in the menu bar.

2 Click the sort option you want:

Sort by Name

Sort by Type

Sort by Date

Sort by Size

Note

You can also choose to sort by date or size. Simply choose the option you want for step 3 (task).

Change the file view

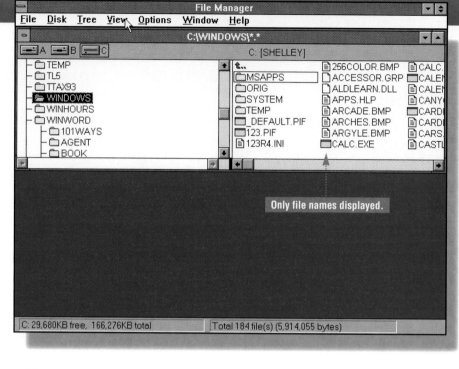

Only file names displayed.

Oops!

Select the View, Name command to return to the original view.

1 **Open the File Manager.**
To open the File Manager, double-click the Main group icon. Then double-click the File Manager icon. For more information on this step, see *TASK: Open the File Manager*.

2 **Click View in the menu bar.**
This step opens the View menu and displays a list of View commands.

3 **Click the All File Details command.**
This step selects the All File Details command. You now see all the file details listed (the name, size, date created, and time created).

After

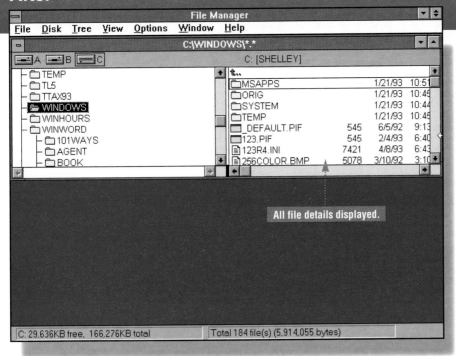

All file details displayed.

REVIEW

1 Click **View** in the menu bar.

2 Click the **All File Details** command.

Note

If you want to select which file details are displayed, select View, Partial Details. Then select the options you want and choose OK.

Display only selected files

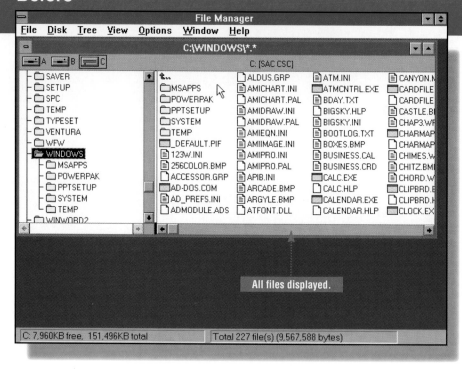

All files displayed.

Oops!

To view all files again, follow this same procedure, but type *.* in the Name text box (step 5). This entry tells Windows to display all files.

1 **Open the File Manager.**
To open the File Manager, double-click the Main group icon. Then double-click the File Manager icon. For more information on this step, see *TASK: Open the File Manager*.

2 **Click the WINDOWS directory.**
This step displays the files and directories in the WINDOWS directory. (The Before screen shows this step.)

You may have to scroll through the list to find WINDOWS. The scroll arrows appear in the middle of the window. To scroll, click the scroll arrow that points in the direction that you want to scroll.

3 **Click View in the menu bar.**
This step opens the View menu. You see the different options for viewing your files.

4 **Click By File Type.**
This step selects the By File Type command. The By File Type dialog box appears, which enables you to specify the file types to include. The insertion point is positioned inside the Name text box. For more information on dialog boxes, see the Basics part of this book.

After

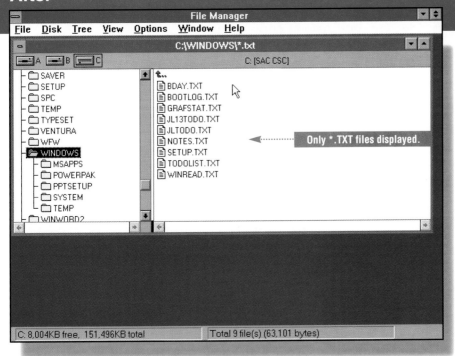

Only *.TXT files displayed.

5 **Type *.txt.**

Typing **.txt* tells Microsoft Windows to display only files with the extension txt. The files can have any name. The * is a wild card, which lets you specify groups of files, rather than naming each individual file.

6 **Click OK.**

This step confirms the selected name. The screen displays all the files in the WINDOWS directory that have the extension TXT.

REVIEW

1 Open the **File Manager**.

2 Click the directory that contains the files you want to display.

3 Click **View** in the menu bar.

4 Click the **By File Type** command.

5 In the Name text box, type the name of the files that you want to include. You can type file names, extensions, or wild cards.

6 Click **OK**.

Select a file

Oops!

If you click the wrong file, deselect the file by clicking on another file.

1 **Open the File Manager.**
To open the File Manager, double-click the Main group icon. Then double-click the File Manager icon. For more information on this step, see *TASK: Open the File Manager*.

The Directory Tree window appears. This window lists the directories in the root (or main) directory of drive C.

2 **Double-click the WINDOWS directory.**
This step displays the files and directories in the WINDOWS directory. (The Before screen shows this step.)

You may have to scroll through the list to find WINDOWS. The scroll arrows appear on the right side of the window. To scroll, click the scroll arrow that points in the direction that you want to scroll. To scroll down, for example, click the down scroll arrow.

3 **Point to the file ARCADE.BMP and click the left mouse button.**
This step selects the file ARCADE.BMP. The file is highlighted on-screen. After you select the file, you can perform many operations on it, such as moving it, copying it, deleting it, and so on. See the other tasks in this section for more information.

Your directory listing should include this file. If not, select a file that it does include.

After

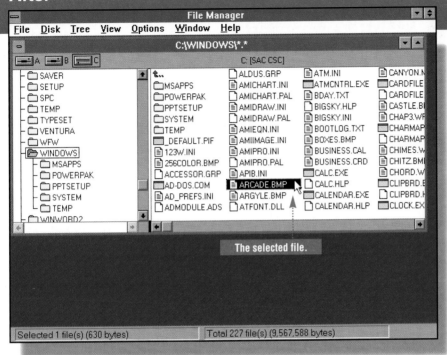

The selected file.

Selected 1 file(s) (630 bytes)   Total 227 file(s) (9,567,588 bytes)

REVIEW

1 Open the **File Manager**.

2 If necessary, expand the directory listing to display the directory that contains the file you want.

3 Double-click the directory that contains the file.

4 Click the file name.

Note

You also can select multiple files. See *TASK: Select multiple files*.

Select multiple files

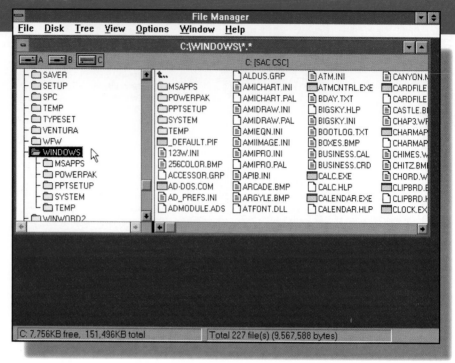

Oops!

To deselect a file, press and hold the Ctrl key and click the file.

1 **Open the File Manager.**
To open the File Manager, double-click the Main group icon to open the Main program group window. Then double-click the File Manager icon to start the File Manager. For more information on this step, see *TASK: Open the File Manager*.

The Directory Tree window appears. This window lists the directories in the root (or main) directory of drive C.

2 **Double-click the WINDOWS directory.**
This step displays the files and directories in the WINDOWS directory. (The Before screen shows this step.)

You may have to scroll through the list to find WINDOWS. The scroll arrows appear on the right side of the window. To scroll, click the scroll arrow that points in the direction that you want to scroll. To scroll down, for example, click the down scroll arrow.

3 **Point to the file ARCADE.BMP and click the mouse button.**
This step selects the ARCADE.BMP file. The file highlights on-screen. Your directory listing should include this file. If not, select a file that it does include.

4 **Point to the file ARGYLE.BMP.**
ARGYLE.BMP is the next file that you want to select. Your directory listing should include this file. If not, select a file that it does include.

After

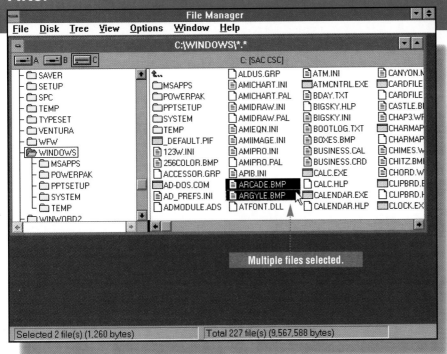

Multiple files selected.

Selected 2 file(s) (1,260 bytes) | Total 227 file(s) (9,567,588 bytes)

5 **Press and hold the Ctrl key and click the mouse button.**
This step selects the second file without deselecting the first file.
You can continue this process to select many files. After you select
the files, you can perform operations on them. See the other tasks
in this section for instructions.

REVIEW

1 Open the **File Manager**.

2 If necessary, expand the directory listing to display the directory
that contains the file you want.

3 Double-click the directory that contains the file.

4 Click the first file name.

5 Point to the next file.

6 Press and hold the **Ctrl** key and click the mouse button.

7 Repeat steps 5 and 6 until you select all the files that you want.

Note

To select all files, click
File in the menu bar
and then click the
Select All command.

Note

Select a continuous set
of files by clicking on
the first file, pressing
and holding the Shift
key, and clicking on
the last file.

Select multiple files **103**

Before

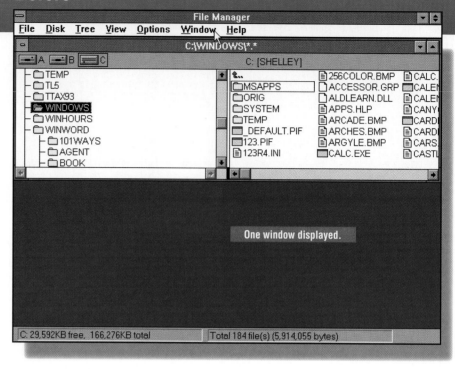

Open two windows

Oops!

To close a window, double-click the Control menu box for the window.

1 **Open the File Manager.**
To open the File Manager, double-click the Main group icon. Then double-click the File Manager icon. For more information on this step, see *TASK: Open the File Manager*.

2 **Click Window in the menu bar.**
This step opens the Window menu and displays a list of Window commands.

3 **Click the New Window command.**
This step selects the New Window command. Now you see two windows of drive C. You can change what is displayed in each window.

After

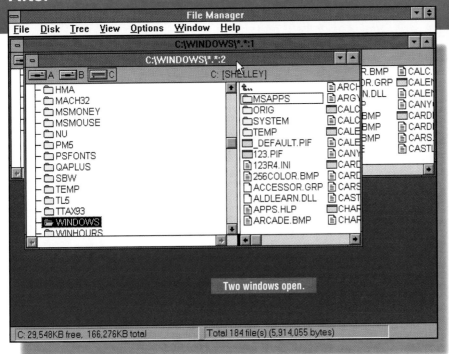

Two windows open.

SHORTCUT

Double-click the drive icon you want to display to open a second window. For example, if you are currently displaying drive C and you want to open a second window that shows drive B, double-click the drive B icon.

REVIEW

1 Click **Window** in the menu bar.

2 Click the **New Window** command.

Note

Opening two windows is useful when you want to move and copy files from directory to directory or from one disk to another.

Tile the windows

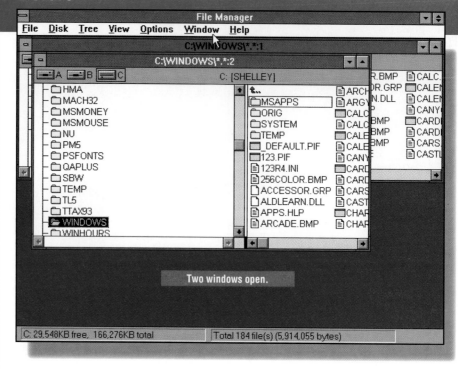

Oops!

To close a window, double-click the Control menu box for the window.

1 **Open the File Manager.**
To open the File Manager, double-click the Main group icon. Then double-click the File Manager icon. For more information on this step, see *TASK: Open the File Manager*.

2 **Click Window in the menu bar.**
This step opens the Window menu and displays a list of Window commands.

3 **Click the Tile command.**
This step selects the Tile command. Now you can see both windows.

After

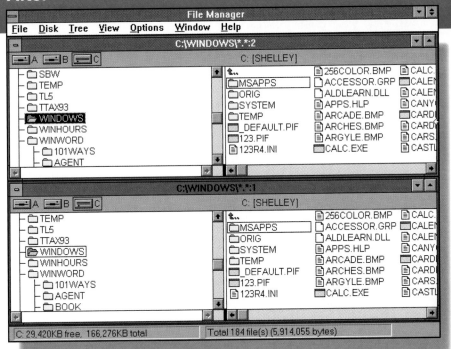

The windows tiled.

REVIEW

1 Click **Window** in the menu bar.

2 Click the **Tile** command.

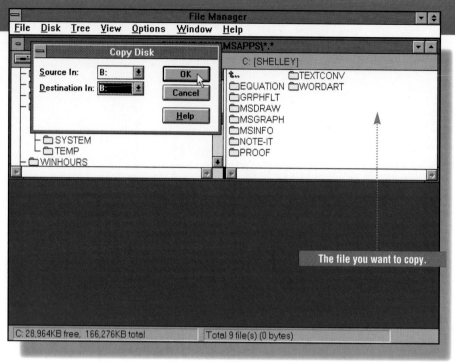

The file you want to copy.

Copy a file

C: [SHELLEY]

TEXTCONV
EQUATION   WORDART
GRPHFLT
MSDRAW
MSGRAPH
MSINFO
NOTE-IT
PROOF

SYSTEM
TEMP
WINHOURS

C: 28,964KB free, 166,276KB total   Total 9 file(s) (0 bytes)

If you change your mind, click Cancel for step 7 (in the task section).

1 **Open the File Manager.**
For more information, see *TASK: Open the File Manager*.

The Directory Tree window appears. This window lists the directories in the root (or main) directory of drive C.

2 **Double-click the WINDOWS directory.**
This step displays the files and directories in the WINDOWS directory. You may have to scroll through the list to find WINDOWS.

3 **Point to the file README.WRI and click the mouse button.**
This step selects the file README.WRI. (The Before screen shows this step.) If your directory listing doesn't include this file, select a different file.

4 **Click File in the menu bar.**
This step opens the File menu. You see a list of File commands.

5 **Click Copy.**
This step selects the Copy command. The Copy dialog box appears. The text box named From: displays the selected file. The insertion point is positioned inside the To: box, where you enter the name for the copy that you are creating.

After

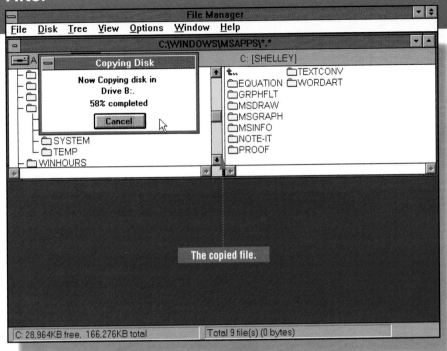

The copied file.

---

6 **Type DOC.WRI.**
DOC.WRI is the name of the file that you want to create. You will have two copies of the same file: README.WRI and DOC.WRI. Both copies will be stored in the same directory.

7 **Click OK.**
This step makes a copy of the file. In the directory listing, you see the new file. (You may need to scroll.)

REVIEW

1 Open the **File Manager**.

2 If necessary, expand the directory listing to display the directory that contains the file you want to copy.

3 Double-click the directory that contains the file.

4 Click the name of the file that you want to copy.

5 Click **File** in the menu bar.

6 Click the **Copy** command.

7 Type the new file's name in the To: text box.

8 Press **Enter**.

> **Note**
>
> You can copy the file to a different drive or directory by typing the path name (drive, directory, and file name) in step 7.

> **Note**
>
> If you want to copy the file to another directory (and keep the same name), press and hold down the Ctrl key. Then click and hold down the mouse; drag the file from the file list to the directory where you want the copy. (It may be easier to open two windows and drag the file from one window to another.)

Delete a file

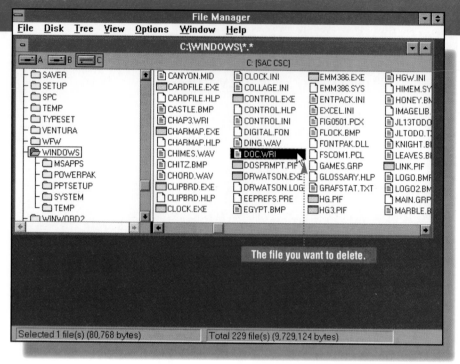

File Manager

<u>F</u>ile <u>D</u>isk <u>T</u>ree <u>V</u>iew <u>O</u>ptions <u>W</u>indow <u>H</u>elp

C:\WINDOWS*.*

C: [SAC CSC]

SAVER	CANYON.MID	CLOCK.INI	EMM386.EXE	HGW.INI
SETUP	CARDFILE.EXE	COLLAGE.INI	EMM386.SYS	HIMEM.SY
SPC	CARDFILE.HLP	CONTROL.EXE	ENTPACK.INI	HONEY.BN
TEMP	CASTLE.BMP	CONTROL.HLP	EXCEL.INI	IMAGELIB.
TYPESET	CHAP3.WRI	CONTROL.INI	FIG0501.PCX	JL13TODO
VENTURA	CHARMAP.EXE	DIGITAL.FON	FLOCK.BMP	JLTODO.T:
WFW	CHARMAP.HLP	DING.WAV	FONTPAK.DLL	KNIGHT.BI
WINDOWS	CHIMES.WAV	DOC.WRI	FSCOM1.PCL	LEAVES.BI
MSAPPS	CHITZ.BMP	DOSPRMPT.PIF	GAMES.GRP	LINK.PIF
POWERPAK	CHORD.WAV	DRWATSON.EXE	GLOSSARY.HLP	LOGO.BMF
PPTSETUP	CLIPBRD.EXE	DRWATSON.LOG	GRAFSTAT.TXT	LOGO2.BM
SYSTEM	CLIPBRD.HLP	EEPREFS.PRE	HG.PIF	MAIN.GRP
TEMP	CLOCK.EXE	EGYPT.BMP	HG3.PIF	MARBLE.B
WINWORD2				

The file you want to delete.

Selected 1 file(s) (80,768 bytes)   Total 229 file(s) (9,729,124 bytes)

Oops!

If you change your mind about deleting a file, click Cancel in step 7.

1 **Open the File Manager.**
For more information, see *TASK: Open the File Manager*.

The Directory Tree window appears. This window lists the directories in the root (or main) directory of drive C.

2 **Double-click the WINDOWS directory.**
This step displays the files and directories in the WINDOWS directory. You may have to scroll through the list to find WINDOWS.

3 **Point to the file DOC.WRI and click the mouse button.**
This step selects the DOC.WRI file. (The Before screen shows this step.) If you followed the exercise (in *TASK:Copy a file*) for copying a file, you should have this file. If you don't have the DOC.WR1 file, select a file that you do not need.

4 **Click File in the menu bar.**
This step opens the File menu. You see a list of File commands.

5 **Click Delete.**
This step selects the Delete command. The Delete dialog box appears. The selected file appears in the text box.

6 **Click OK.**
This step starts to delete the selected file. You see an alert box that says Delete file C:\WINDOWS\DOC.WRI?

After

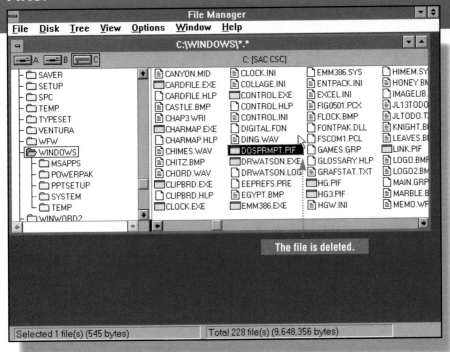

The file is deleted.

Selected 1 file(s) (545 bytes)   Total 228 file(s) (9,648,356 bytes)

7 **Click Yes.**
Clicking on Yes confirms that you want to delete the file.

REVIEW

1 Open the **File Manager**.

2 If necessary, expand the directory listing to display the directory that contains the file you want.

3 Double-click the directory that contains the file.

4 Click the file name that you want to delete.

5 Click **File** in the menu bar.

6 Click the **Delete** command.

7 Click the **OK** button.

8 Click **Yes.**

SHORTCUT

You also can press Del to select the File Delete command.

Note

Make sure that you don't delete files that you need. You cannot undelete files in Microsoft Windows..

Rename a file

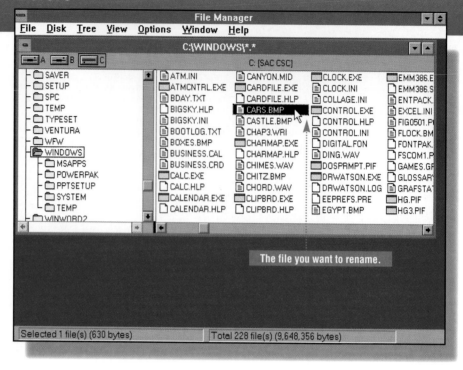

The file you want to rename.

Oops!

If you change your mind about renaming the file, click Cancel in the Rename dialog box before you press Enter. To rename the file its original name, follow this same procedure.

1 **Open the File Manager.**
For more information, see *TASK: Open the File Manager*.

2 **Double-click the WINDOWS directory.**
Double-clicking displays the files and directories in the WINDOWS directory. You may have to scroll through the list to find WINDOWS. The scroll arrows appear on the right side of the window. To scroll, click the scroll arrow that points in the direction that you want to scroll. To scroll down, for example, click the down scroll arrow.

3 **Point to the file CARS.BMP and click the mouse button.**
This step selects the file CARS.BMP. The file is highlighted on-screen.

4 **Click File in the menu bar.**
This step opens the File menu. You see a list of File commands.

5 **Click Rename.**
This step selects the Rename command. The Rename dialog box appears. Inside this dialog box, you see the current directory name and two text boxes. The first text box is named From and displays the selected file. The second text box is named To. The insertion point is positioned inside the To: box, and you type the new file name in this box.

After

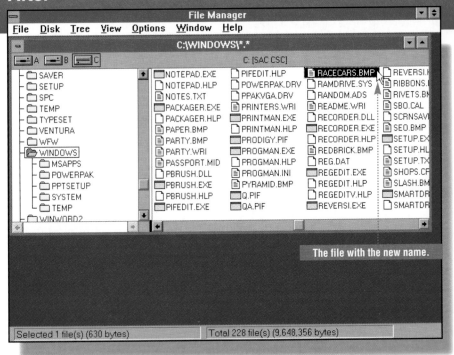

The file with the new name.

Selected 1 file(s) (630 bytes)   Total 228 file(s) (9,648,356 bytes)

6 **Type RACECARS.BMP.**
RACECARS.BMP is the new name that you want to assign the file.

7 **Click OK.**
Pressing OK confirms the new name. The file appears in the current directory listing under its new name.

REVIEW

1 Open the **File Manager**.

2 If necessary, expand the directory listing to display the directory that contains the file you want.

3 Double-click the directory that contains the file.

4 Click the name of the file that you want to rename.

5 Click **File** in the menu bar.

6 Click the **Rename** command.

7 Type the new name in the To text box.

8 Click **OK**.

Note

Don't rename a file that must have a certain name. For example, don't rename any program files (files with the extension COM, EXE, PIF, or BAT).

Move a file

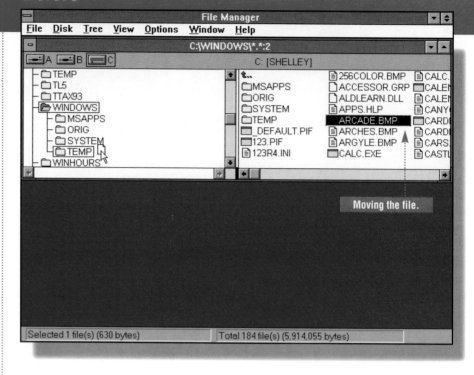

File Manager

File Disk Tree View Options Window Help

C:\WINDOWS*.*:2

A B C   C: [SHELLEY]

- TEMP
- TL5
- TTAX93
- WINDOWS
  - MSAPPS
  - ORIG
  - SYSTEM
  - TEMP
- WINHOURS

t..
MSAPPS
ORIG
SYSTEM
TEMP
_DEFAULT.PIF
123.PIF
123R4.INI

256COLOR.BMP   CALC.
ACCESSOR.GRP   CALE
ALDLEARN.DLL   CALE
APPS.HLP   CANY
ARCADE.BMP   CARD
ARCHES.BMP   CARD
ARGYLE.BMP   CARS
CALC.EXE   CASTL

Moving the file.

Selected 1 file(s) (630 bytes)   Total 184 file(s) (5,914,055 bytes)

Oops!

If you change your mind, click Cancel for step 6. Follow this same procedure to move the file back to its original location.

1 **Open the File Manager.**
To open the File Manager, double-click the Main group icon. Then double-click the File Manager icon. For more information on this step, see *TASK: Open the File Manager*.

2 **Click the WINDOWS directory.**
This step displays the files and directories in the WINDOWS directory.

You may have to scroll through the list to find WINDOWS.

3 **Point to the file ARCADE.BMP and click the mouse button.**
This step selects the file, and the file is highlighted on-screen. Your directory listing should include this file. If not, select a file that it does include. You may have to scroll the window to find the file.

4 **Drag the file to the TEMP directory.**
This step tells Windows to move the file to the directory. Drag from the file list to the directory list on the left. You see a message that asks you to confirm the move.

5 **Click Yes.**
This step confirms the move.

The entry no longer appears in the current directory listing.

After

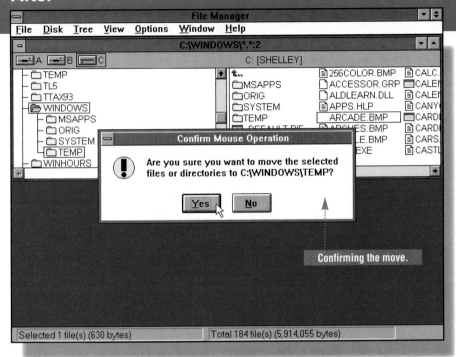

Confirming the move.

Note

You can also use the menu to move files. Click the file you want. Select the File Move command. Type the path and name for the file. Click OK.

Note

Do not move a file that must be in a specific directory. For example, don't move any program files (files with the extension COM,

REVIEW

1 Open the **File Manager**.

2 If necessary, expand the directory listing to display the directory that contains the file you want.

3 Click the directory that contains the file.

4 Click the name of the file that you want to move.

5 Drag the file to the directory you want.

6 Click **Yes**.

Search for a file

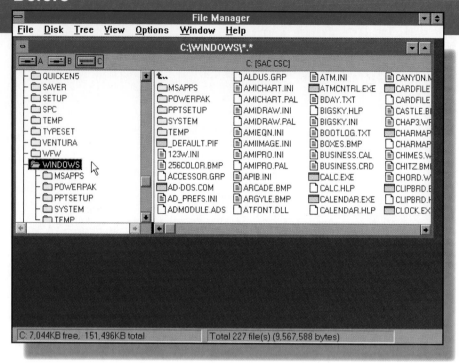

QUICKEN5
SAVER
SETUP
SPC
TEMP
TYPESET
VENTURA
WFW
WINDOWS
  MSAPPS
  POWERPAK
  PPTSETUP
  SYSTEM
  TEMP

t..
MSAPPS
POWERPAK
PPTSETUP
SYSTEM
TEMP
_DEFAULT.PIF
123W.INI
256COLOR.BMP
ACCESSOR.GRP
AD-DOS.COM
AD_PREFS.INI
ADMODULE.ADS

ALDUS.GRP
AMICHART.INI
AMICHART.PAL
AMIDRAW.INI
AMIDRAW.PAL
AMIEQN.INI
AMIIMAGE.INI
AMIPRO.INI
AMIPRO.PAL
APIB.INI
ARCADE.BMP
ARGYLE.BMP
ATFONT.DLL

ATM.INI
ATMCNTRL.EXE
BDAY.TXT
BIGSKY.HLP
BIGSKY.INI
BOOTLOG.TXT
BOXES.BMP
BUSINESS.CAL
BUSINESS.CRD
CALC.EXE
CALC.HLP
CALENDAR.EXE
CALENDAR.HLP

CANYON.N
CARDFILE
CARDFILE
CASTLE.BI
CHAP3.WF
CHARMAP
CHARMAP
CHIMES.W
CHITZ.BMI
CHORD.W
CLIPBRD.E
CLIPBRD.H
CLOCK.EX

C: 7,044KB free, 151,496KB total   Total 227 file(s) (9,567,588 bytes)

Oops!

If the search does not find the requested file, you may have typed the name incorrectly. Try again.

1 **Open the File Manager.**
To open the File Manager, double-click the Main group icon. Then double-click the File Manager icon. For more information on this step, see *TASK: Open the File Manager*.

2 **Click File in the menu bar.**
This step opens the File menu. You see a list of File commands.

3 **Click Search.**
This step selects the Search command. The Search dialog box appears. The Search For text box may contain *.*. (The insertion point is positioned inside this box.) The second box, Start From, lists the current directory. Also notice the Search All Subdirectories box. When this box contains an X, Windows searches all subdirectories.

4 **Type CLOCK.EXE.**
CLOCK.EXE is the name of the file that you want to find. If you do not know the entire name of the file, you can use wild cards in the search. For example, you could specify this file by typing CLOCK.*. Microsoft Windows would find every file named CLOCK, regardless of the file extension.

5 **Click OK.**
This step confirms the name and starts the search. Windows looks through all directories for files that match this name. When it finds

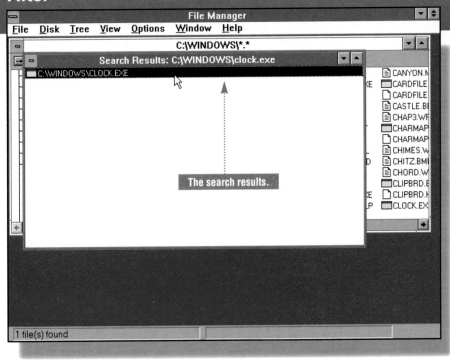

File Manager

<u>F</u>ile <u>D</u>isk <u>T</u>ree <u>V</u>iew <u>O</u>ptions <u>W</u>indow <u>H</u>elp

C:\WINDOWS*.*

Search Results: C:\WINDOWS\clock.exe

C:\WINDOWS\CLOCK.EXE

CANYON.N
CARDFILE
CARDFILE
CASTLE.BI
CHAP3.WF
CHARMAP
CHARMAP
CHIMES.W
CHITZ.BMI
CHORD.W
CLIPBRD.E
CLIPBRD.H
CLOCK.EX

The search results.

1 file(s) found

a file, it displays the Search Results window. You see
C:\WINDOWS\CLOCK.EXE, which tells you the location or path
to the file. CLOCK.EXE is stored in the WINDOWS directory on drive C.

For other searches, Windows may find several entries. All matching
entries are listed.

6 **Double-click the Control menu box for this window.**
This step closes the Search Results window.

REVIEW

1 Open the **File Manager**.

2 Click **File** in the menu bar.

3 Click the **Search** command.

4 Type the file name that you want to find. You can use wild cards.

5 Click **OK**.

6 Double-click the **Control menu box** for the Search Results window
to close the window.

Note

A wild card is a
character that lets you
specify a group of files.
For more information,
see your Windows
manual or *Using
Windows 3.1,* Special
Edition.

Create a directory

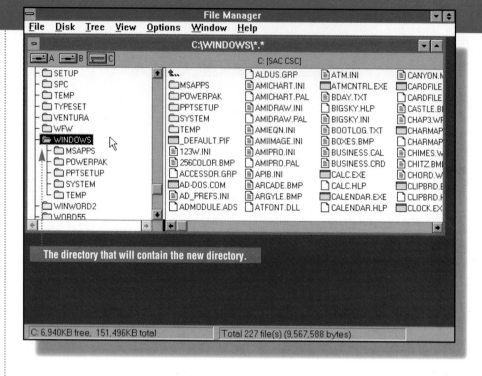

The directory that will contain the new directory.

1 **Open the File Manager.**
To open the File Manager, double-click the Main group icon. Then double-click the File Manager icon. For more information on this step, see *TASK: Open the File Manager*.

2 **Click the WINDOWS directory.**
This step selects WINDOWS as the current directory. (The Before screen shows this step.) You may have to scroll through the list to find WINDOWS.

3 **Click File in the menu bar.**
This step opens the File menu. You see a list of File commands.

4 **Click Create Directory.**
This step displays the Create Directory dialog box. This dialog box lists the current directory name and contains the Name text box. The insertion point is positioned inside this text box.

5 **Type DATA.**
DATA is the name of the directory that you want to create. This directory will be a subdirectory of the WINDOWS directory.

6 **Click OK.**
This step confirms the name and creates the directory.

After

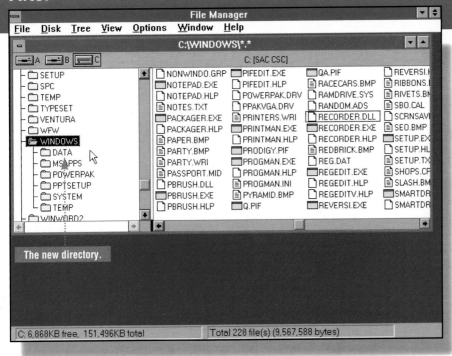

The new directory.

REVIEW

1 Open the **File Manager**.

2 Click the directory in which you want to place the new directory. Click **C:** to select the root directory.

3 Click **File** in the menu bar.

4 Click the **Create Directory** command.

5 Type the directory name.

6 Click **OK**.

Note

If you want to make the directory a branch of the root directory, select C:\ in the Directory Tree window.

Create a directory

Before

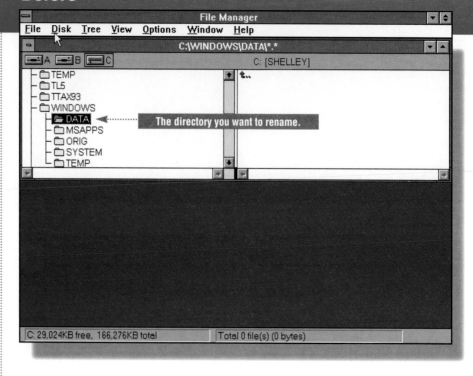

Rename a directory

Oops!

If you change your mind about renaming the file, click Cancel in the Rename dialog box before you press Enter. To rename the file its original name, follow this same procedure.

1 **Open the File Manager.**
To open the File Manager, double-click the Main group icon. Then double-click the File Manager icon. For more information on this step, see *TASK: Open the File Manager*.

2 **Click the DATA directory.**
This step selects the directory you want to rename. If you followed the Task: Create a directory, you should have this directory. If you didn't, select a directory you do have.

3 **Click File in the menu bar.**
This step opens the File menu. You see a list of File commands.

4 **Click Rename.**
This step selects the Rename command. The Rename dialog box appears. Inside this dialog box, you see the current directory name and two text boxes. The first text box is named From and displays the selected directory. The second text box is named To. The insertion point is positioned inside the To box, and you type the new name in this box.

5 **Type DOCS.**
DOCS is the new name that you want to assign the directory.

6 **Click OK.**
This step confirms the new name.

After

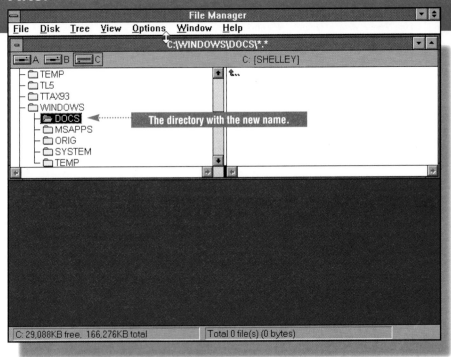

File Manager

File Disk Tree View Options Window Help

C:\WINDOWS\DOCS*.*

A B C   C: [SHELLEY]

```
─ TEMP
─ TL5
─ TTAX93
─ WINDOWS
    DOCS  ◄----- The directory with the new name.
    ─ MSAPPS
    ─ ORIG
    ─ SYSTEM
    ─ TEMP
```

C: 29,088KB free, 166,276KB total   Total 0 file(s) (0 bytes)

REVIEW

1 Open the **File Manager**.

2 Click the directory you want to rename.

3 Click **File** in the menu bar.

4 Click the **Rename** command.

5 Type the new name in the To text box.

6 Click **OK**.

Move a directory

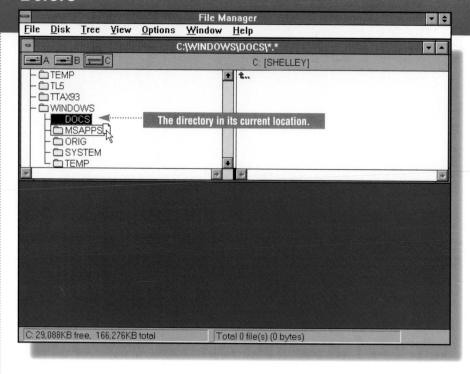

File Manager

File Disk Tree View Options Window Help

C:\WINDOWS\DOCS*.*

A B C   C: [SHELLEY]

- TEMP
- TL5
- TTAX93
- WINDOWS
    DOCS ◄........ The directory in its current location.
    MSAPPS
    ORIG
    SYSTEM
    TEMP

C: 29,088KB free, 166,276KB total   Total 0 file(s) (0 bytes)

Oops!

Follow this same procedure to move the directory back to the original location.

1 Open the File Manager.

To open the File Manager, double-click the Main group icon. Then double-click the File Manager icon. For more information on this step, see *TASK: Open the File Manager*.

2 Click the DOCS directory. Hold down the mouse button and drag the directory to the MSAPPSdirectory.

This step moves the directory to the MSAPPS directory. You see a message asking you to confirm the move.

3 Click Yes.

This step completes the move.

After

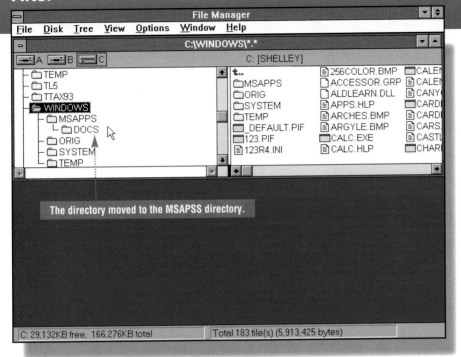

The directory moved to the MSAPSS directory.

REVIEW

1 Drag the directory to the new location.

2 Click **Yes**.

Remove a directory

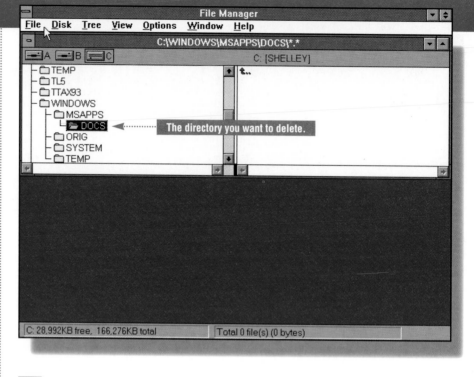

File Manager

File Disk Tree View Options Window Help

C:\WINDOWS\MSAPPS\DOCS*.*

A B C   C: [SHELLEY]

- TEMP
- TL5
- TTAX93
- WINDOWS
  - MSAPPS
    - DOCS ◀········· The directory you want to delete.
  - ORIG
  - SYSTEM
  - TEMP

C: 28,992KB free, 166,276KB total   Total 0 file(s) (0 bytes)

Oops!

If you are unsure
whether you want to
remove the directory,
click Cancel in step 4
or step 5 of the task
section.

1 **Open the File Manager.**
To open the File Manager, double-click the Main group icon. Then
double-click the File Manager icon. For more information on this
step, see *TASK: Open the File Manager*.

2 **Click the DOCS directory.**
DOCS is the directory that you want to delete. If you don't have this
directory, select one that you do have. Be sure to select a directory
that you do not need.

The DOCS directory should be empty. If not, you may want to
create an empty directory for this exercise. See *TASK: Create a
directory*.

You cannot remove a directory unless all the files in that directory
are deleted. If the directory contains files or other directories and
you try to delete it, Windows prompts you to confirm the deletion
of each file and directory. You must answer Yes and delete all files
and directories before the directory is removed.

3 **Click File in the menu bar.**
This step opens the File menu. You see a list of File commands.

4 **Click Delete.**
This step displays the Delete dialog box. The directory name is
listed in this box.

After

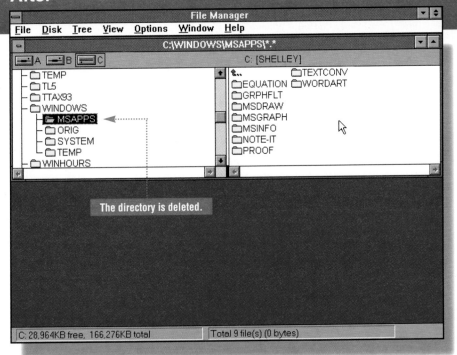

5 **Click OK.**
This step tells Windows that you want to delete the selected directory. You see an alert box that asks you to confirm deleting the directory.

6 **Click Yes.**
Clicking on Yes confirms the removal of the directory.

REVIEW

1 Open the **File Manager**.

2 Select the directory that you want to delete.

3 Click **File** in the menu bar.

4 Click the **Delete** command.

5 Click **OK**.

6 Click the **Yes** button.

Format a diskette

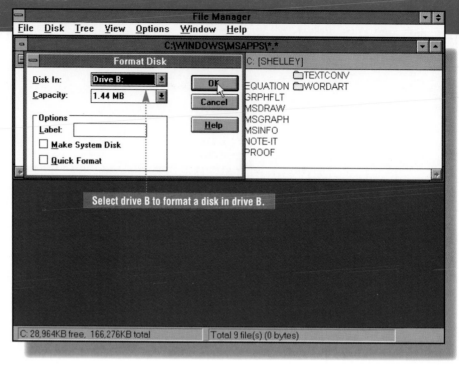

File Manager

File Disk Tree View Options Window Help

C:\WINDOWS\MSAPPS*.*

Format Disk

Disk In: Drive B:

Capacity: 1.44 MB

Options
Label:
☐ Make System Disk
☐ Quick Format

OK
Cancel
Help

C: [SHELLEY]
☐TEXTCONV
EQUATION ☐WORDART
GRPHFLT
MSDRAW
MSGRAPH
MSINFO
NOTE-IT
PROOF

Select drive B to format a disk in drive B.

C: 28,964KB free, 166,276KB total   Total 9 file(s) (0 bytes)

Oops!

To cancel the formatting process, click Cancel in the Formatting dialog box. If you format a disk by mistake, you might be able to use Microsoft DOS 5 or 6 or a third-party utility program such as Norton Utilities to recover the disk. See *Using MS-DOS 6.2, Special Edition.*

1 **Open the File Manager.**
To open the File Manager, double-click the Main group icon. Then double-click the File Manager icon. For more information on this step, see *TASK: Open the File Manager.*

2 **Insert the disk you want to format in drive B.**
Be sure to use a blank disk or a disk you don't need anymore. Formatting erases all the information on the disk.

3 **Click Disk in the menu bar.**
This step opens the Disk menu.

4 **Click the Format Disk command.**
This step selects the Format Disk command. You see the Format Disk dialog box.

5 **Click the Disk In drop-down list; then click drive B.**
This step tells File Manager to format the disk in drive B.

6 **Click the Capacity drop-down list. Then click the correct capacity for the disk in drive B.**

7 **Click OK.**
This step starts the formatting. You see a message that tells you all the information will be deleted. You are asked to confirm that's okay.

After

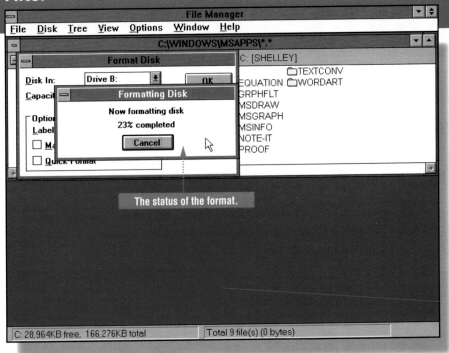

The status of the format.

---

8 **Click Yes.**
The formatting starts. You see the status of the formatting on-screen. When the format is complete, you see a message that asks whether you want to format another disk.

9 **Click No.**
This step tells File Manager you don't want to format another disk.

REVIEW

1 Insert the disk you want to format.

2 Click **Disk** in the menu bar.

3 Click the **Format Disk** command.

4 If necessary, change the Disk In to select which drive contains the disk.

5 If necessary, click the **Capacity** drop-down list. Then click the correct capacity for the disk in drive B.

6 Click **OK**.

7 Click **Yes**. Then click **No**.

Note

Formatting is a process that prepares disks for use. You can buy preformatted disks. If the disks aren't formatted, you have to format them before you can use them.

Copy a diskette

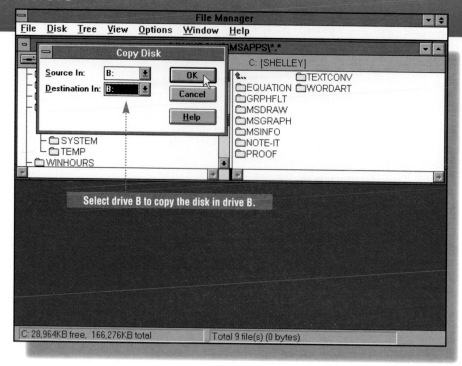

Select drive B to copy the disk in drive B.

Oops!

To cancel the copying process, click Cancel.

1 **Open the File Manager.**
To open the File Manager, double-click the Main group icon. Then double-click the File Manager icon.

2 **Click Disk in the menu bar.**
This step opens the Disk menu.

3 **Click the Copy Disk command.**
This step selects the Copy Disk command. You see the Copy Disk dialog box.

4 **Click the Source In drop-down list; then click drive B.**
This step tells File Manager to copy the disk in drive B.

5 **Click the Destination In drop-down list; then click drive B.**
This step tells File Manager to copy the disk to drive B. Unless you have two drives the same size, you have to select the same drive for the source and destination.

6 **Click OK.**
You are prompted to insert the source disk.

7 **Insert the disk you want to copy in drive B.**
This is the disk you want to copy. You need to have another disk ready. That is the disk that will contain the copy. This disk should be blank or contain information you don't need anymore.

After

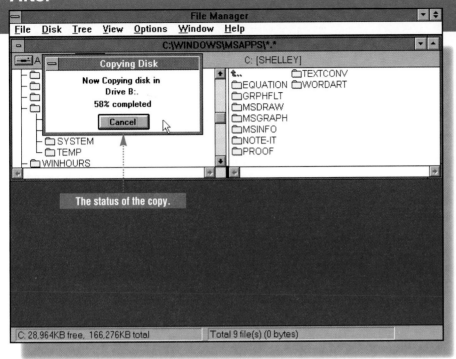

The status of the copy.

8 **Click OK.**
This step starts the copying. You see a message that tells you all the information will be deleted. You are asked to confirm that it is okay.

9 **Click Yes.**
The copying starts. You see the status of the copy on-screen. File Manager prompts you to insert the destination disk.

10 **Insert the destination disk in drive B and click OK.**
This step inserts the disk that will contain the copy.

REVIEW

1 Click **Disk** in the menu bar.

2 Click the **Copy Disk** command.

3 If necessary, change the **Source In** and **Destination In** options to select which drive contains the disk.

4 Click **OK**.

5 Insert the source disk and click **OK.**

6 Insert the destination disk and click **OK**.

Note

You may need to swap the source and destination disks more than once. You are returned to the File Manager when the copy is complete.

Run a program from File Manager

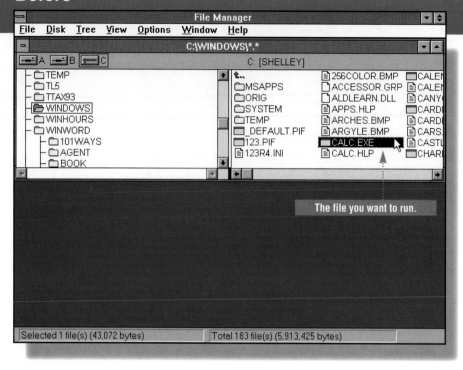

The file you want to run.

Oops!

To exit the program, see *TASK: Exit a program.*

1 Open the File Manager.
To open the File Manager, double-click the Main group icon. Then double-click the File Manager icon. For more information on this step, see *TASK: Open the File Manager.*

2 Click the WINDOWS directory.
This step displays the files in this directory. This directory contains the program you want to start.

3 Double-click the CALC.EXE file.
This step starts the program.

After

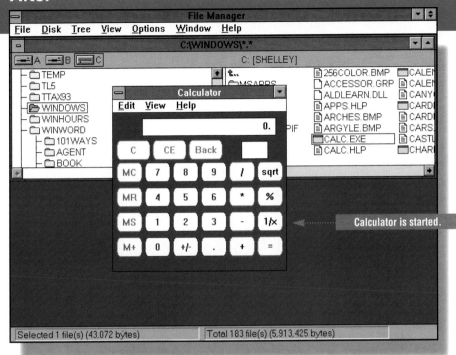

Calculator is started.

REVIEW

Double-click the program file.

Note

Most program files have the extension EXE or COM. For more information on program files, see *Using Windows 3.1*, Special Edition.

Change the font used in the File Manager

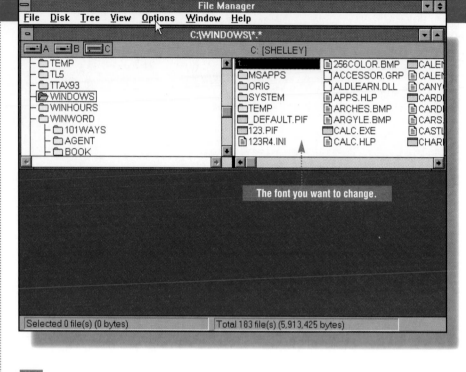

The font you want to change.

Oops!

Follow this same procedure to change back to the original font and font size.

1 **Open the File Manager.**
To open the File Manager, double-click the Main group icon. Then double-click the File Manager icon. For more information on this step, see *TASK: Open the File Manager*.

2 **Click Options in the menu bar.**
This step opens the Options menu and displays a list of Options commands.

3 **Click the Font command.**
This step selects the Font command. You see the Font dialog box.

4 **Click Times New Roman in the Font list.**
This step selects the font you want. You may have to scroll through the Font list to display this font.

5 **Click 12 in the Size list.**
This step selects 12-point type.

6 **Click the Lowercase option.**
This step tells File Manager to display the files in lowercase. (There should be an X in the check box.)

7 **Click OK.**
The directory and file listings are displayed in the new font and size.

After

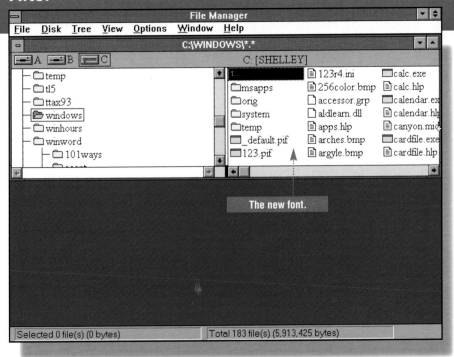

The new font.

Selected 0 file(s) (0 bytes)   Total 183 file(s) (5,913,425 bytes)

REVIEW

1 Click **Options** in the menu bar.

2 Click the **Font** command.

3 In the Font list, click the font you want.

4 In the Size list, click the size you want.

5 If you want to display the files in lowercase, click in the **Lowercase** check box so that there's an X in the box.

6 Click **OK**.

Close the File Manager

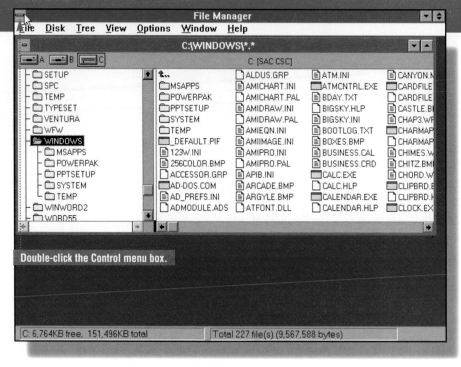

Double-click the Control menu box.

Oops!

To restart the File Manager, see *TASK: Open the File Manager*.

Double-click the **Control menu box** for the File Manager.

This step closes the File Manager.

After

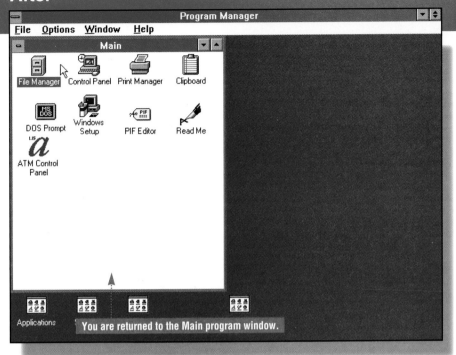

You are returned to the Main program window.

REVIEW

Double-click the **Control menu box.**

Note

Although the Directory Tree window has a Control menu box, you cannot close this window unless you close the File Manager.

Using Write

This section covers the following tasks:

- Start Windows Write
- Type text
- Save a Write document
- Open a Write File
- Add text
- Cut and paste text
- Copy text
- Delete text
- Center text
- Make text bold
- Make text italic
- Change the font
- Change the font size
- Indent text
- Find text
- Print a Write document

Start Windows Write

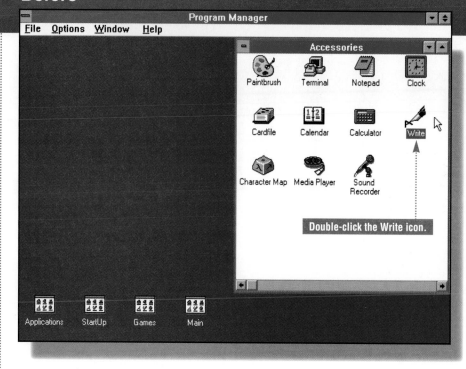

Double-click the Write icon.

Oops!

To exit the program, double-click the Control menu box for the Write window. If you have made changes, you are prompted to save the file.

1 **Double-click the Accessories icon.**
The Write program is stored in the Accessories program group. To start the program, you open the window for that group.

On-screen, you see several icons in a window. The icon for Write looks like a pen stylus.

2 **Double-click the Write icon.**
This step opens the Write program. You see a blank document on-screen. The title bar reminds you of the name of the program (Write) and the document (Untitled). The document remains untitled until you save it.

Notice that Write is a word processing program with its own menu system and help. The program offers many editing and formatting features. This book covers some basic tasks—creating, saving, opening, editing, and printing a document. Including all Write features, however, is beyond the scope of this book. You might want to experiment with what you already know about Microsoft Windows and Microsoft Windows programs. For complete information about the Write program, see *Using Windows 3.1, Special Edition.*

After

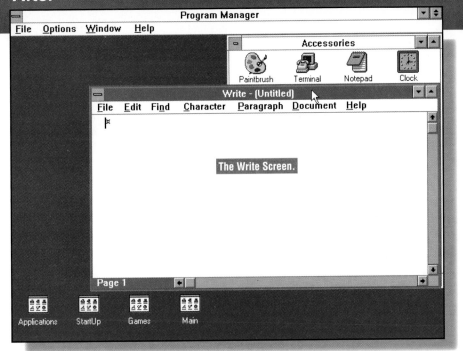

REVIEW

1 Double-click the **Accessories** icon.

2 Double-click the **Write** icon.

Note

To see more of the Write screen, maximize the window. See *TASK: Maximize a window.*

Type text

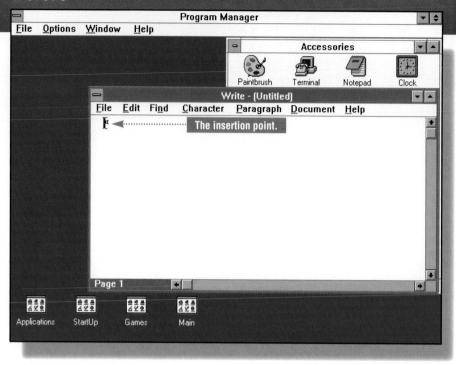

Oops!

To close the document without saving it, click File and then Exit. When prompted to save the current changes, click No.

1 **Start the Write program.**
For information on this task, see *TASK: Start Windows Write*. You see a blank document. The insertion point is blinking on-screen.

2 **Type MEMO.**
MEMO is the first line of the new document.

3 **Press Enter twice.**
Pressing Enter twice ends the line, moves the insertion point to the beginning of the next line, and inserts a blank line.

4 **Type Don't forget that Friday, June 7 is a special company holiday. The office will be closed this day so that we can have a company picnic.**
As you type, the insertion point moves right. When you reach the end of the line, the text automatically moves (or wraps) to the next line. You do not have to press Enter to end a line.

5 **Press Enter twice.**
Pressing Enter twice ends the line, moves the insertion point to the beginning of the next line, and inserts a blank line.

After

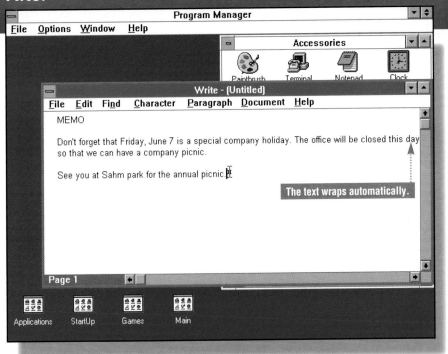

The text wraps automatically.

6 **Type See you at Sahm park for the annual picnic.**
This step completes the text of the document. Remember that Write offers many more features than this simple exercise shows. You can copy text, move text, make text bold, and perform many other editing and formatting tasks. For complete information, see *Using Windows 3.1,* Special Edition.

To see all the text, you might have to resize the window. The After screen shows a resized window. (See *TASK: Resize a window.*)

REVIEW

1 Start the **Write** program.

2 Type the text.

Note

Depending on your printer and the typefaces that you selected, your lines may break differently than those in the After screen.

Note

If the text does not appear clearly (the text is not sharp), you should select a different typeface. See *Using Windows 3.1,* Special Edition, for more information.

Save a Write document

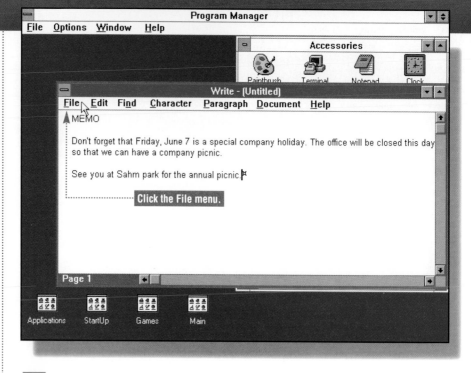

Click the File menu.

Oops!

Be sure to save the file before you close the program. If you don't save, Microsoft Windows prompts you to do so.

1 **Start the Write program.**
For information on this step, see *TASK: Start Windows Write*.

2 **Create a document.**
See *TASK: Create a Write document* for help with this step.

3 **Click the File menu.**
This step opens the File menu. You see a list of File commands.

4 **Click Save.**
This step selects the Save command and displays the File Save As dialog box. Inside this dialog box, you see a File Name text box. (The insertion point is positioned inside this box.) The current directory and a list of directories also are listed in the dialog box.

5 **Type MEMO.**
MEMO is the name that you want to assign the document. The document name can be as many as eight characters long and cannot have any spaces. As a general rule, use only alphanumeric characters.

6 **Click OK.**
This step saves the file. The file is saved with the extension WRI. The file remains on-screen, and the name appears in the title bar.

To open a file that you have saved, see *TASK: Open a Write document*. To clear the current document and create a new document, click File and then New.

After

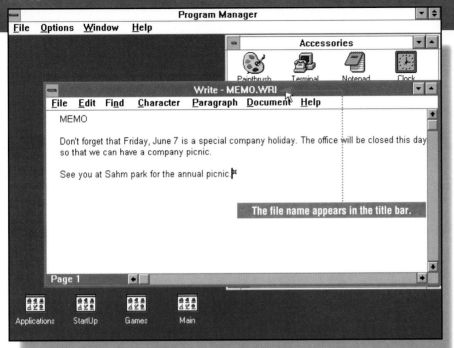

The file name appears in the title bar.

Note

If you have created the document already, skip steps 1 and 2. Start with step 3.

REVIEW

1 Open the **Write** program.

2 Create a document.

3 Click the **Save** command.

4 If you have not saved the file already, type a file name.

5 Click **OK**.

Note

After you have saved a file for the first time, click File and then Save to save the file again. The updated file is saved with the same name.

Open a Write File

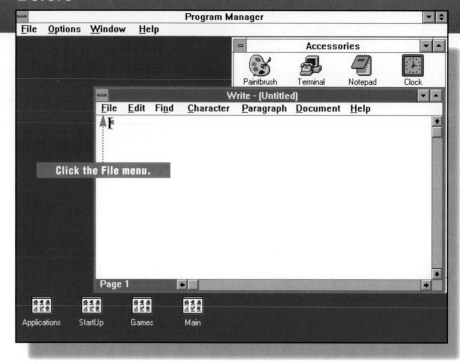

Click the File menu.

Oops!

To close the Write program, save the document and then double-click the Control menu box for the Write window.

1 **Start the Write program.**
For information on this step, See *TASK: Start Windows Write*.

2 **Click File.**
This step opens the File menu. You see a list of File commands.

3 **Click Open.**
This step selects the Open command. You see the File Open dialog box. This dialog box includes a Filename text box. (The insertion point is positioned inside this text box.) The current directory also is listed in the dialog box. You see a Files list and a Directory list.

4 **Type MEMO.**
MEMO is the name of the file you want to open. You also can point to the file name in the Files list box and click the mouse button to select the file.

5 **Click OK.**
Pressing Enter confirms the file name. You see the document on-screen. You now can make any editing or formatting changes.
To save the document, click File and then Save.

After

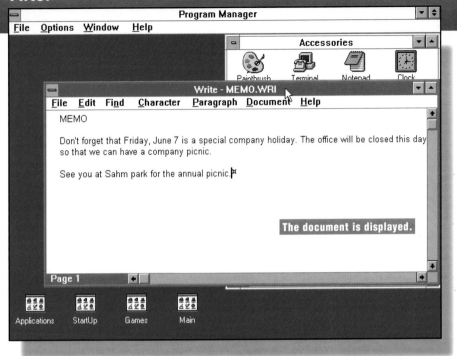

The document is displayed.

REVIEW

1 Start the **Write** program.

2 Click **File** to open the File menu.

3 Click **Open** to select the Open command.

4 Type the name of the file that you want to open.

5 Click **OK**.

SHORTCUT

You also can select and open a file by double-clicking on the file name in the Files box.

Add text

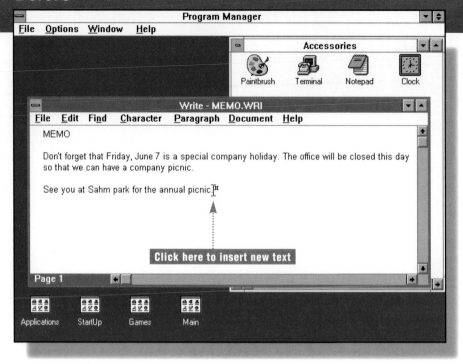

Oops!

If you don't like the edited document, don't save the changes.

1 **Open the MEMO document file.**
For help with this step, see *TASK: Open a Write document*. You see the document on-screen.

If you have not created this document, open a document that you have created.

2 **Click after the last sentence.**
This step positions the insertion point at the location where you want to insert text. The last sentence of the MEMO document that you created previously is *See you at Sahm park for the annual picnic*.

3 **Press Enter twice.**
Pressing Enter twice ends the current line, inserts a blank line, and moves the insertion point to the beginning of the next line.

4 **Type Remember that it's a pitch in. Here are some suggestions on what to bring:.**

5 **Press Enter twice.**
Pressing Enter twice ends the current line, inserts a blank line, and moves the insertion point to the beginning of the next line.

After

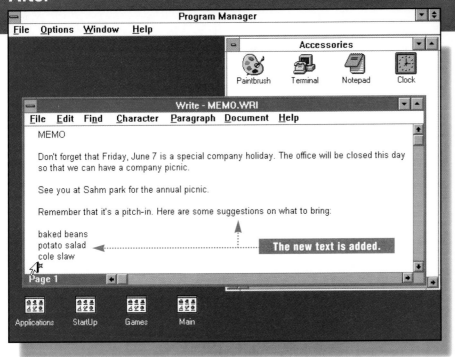

6 Type the following items, pressing Enter after each one:

   baked beans

   potato salad

   cole slaw

7 Save the document.
For help with this step, see *TASK: Save a Write document*.

REVIEW

1 Place the insertion point where you want to add text.

2 Type the text.

3 Click on **File** in the menu bar and then **Save** to save the file.

Cut and paste text

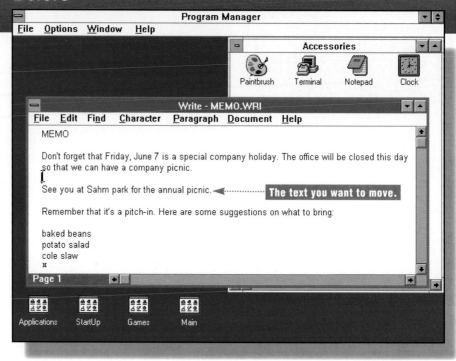

Oops!

You may have to straighten the text some (insert spaces or carriage returns) so that the paragraph breaks are correct.

1 **Open the MEMO document file.**
If the document is already open, you can skip this step. If you have not created this document, open a document that you have created.

2 **Click the blank line before the sentence that begins with the words *See you at*.**
This step positions the insertion point at the beginning of the text that you want to cut.

3 **Press and hold the mouse button, then drag the mouse until you highlight the entire sentence, ending with the period.**
This step highlights the section of text that you want to cut. Be sure that you include the blank line preceding the sentence.

4 **Click Edit in the menu bar.**
This step opens the Edit menu. You see a list of Edit commands.

5 **Click Cut.**
This step selects the Cut command. The text is cut (removed) from the document and stored in a temporary holding place called the Clipboard.

6 **Click the blank line after *cole slaw*.**
This is the place where you want to insert the cut text.

7 **Click Edit in the menu bar.**
This step opens the Edit menu.

After

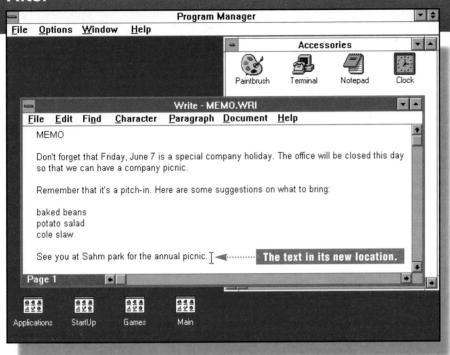

The text in its new location.

---

8 **Click Paste.**
This step selects the Paste command and pastes (inserts) the cut text at the insertion point location.

9 **Save the document.**
For help with this step, see *TASK: Save a Write document*.

REVIEW

1 Select the text that you want to cut.

2 Click **Edit** in the menu bar.

3 Click the **Cut** command.

4 Move the insertion point to the location where you want the text to appear.

5 Click **Edit** in the menu bar.

6 Click **Paste**.

Note

Be sure not to cut anything else before you paste. If you cut or copy other text, the new text replaces the original text in the Clipboard.

Note

You can cut and paste data between documents and between different programs. See *Using Windows 3.1*, Special Edition.

Copy text

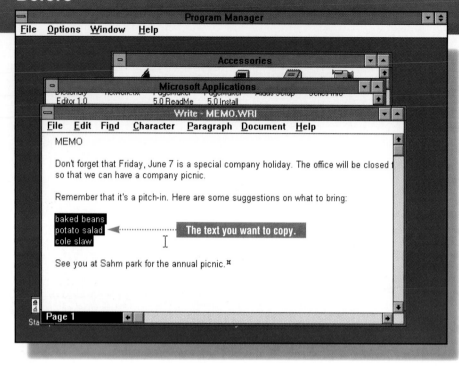

The text you want to copy.

Oops!

To delete the text, see
TASK: Delete text.

1 **Open the MEMO document file.**
If the document is already open, you can skip this step. If you have not created this document, open a document that you have created.

2 **Click before the *b* in *baked beans*.**
This step positions the insertion point at the beginning of the text you want to copy.

3 **Press and hold the mouse button, then drag the mouse until you highlight this line and the next two lines.**
This step highlights the section of text that you want to copy.

4 **Click Edit in the menu bar.**
This step opens the Edit menu. You see a list of Edit commands.

5 **Click Copy.**
This step selects the Copy command. The text is stored in a temporary holding place called the *Clipboard*.

6 **Click before the *b* in *baked beans*.**
This step places the insertion point where you want to add the copy.

7 **Click Edit in the menu bar.**
This step opens the Edit menu.

After

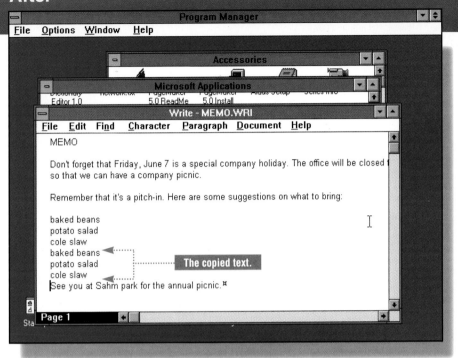

The copied text.

8 **Click Paste.**
This step selects the Paste command and pastes (inserts) the text at that location.

9 **Save the document.**
For help with this step, see *TASK: Save a Write document*.

REVIEW

1 Select the text that you want to copy.

2 Click **Edit** in the menu bar.

3 Click the **Copy** command.

4 Move the insertion point to the location where you want the text to appear.

5 Click **Edit** in the menu bar.

6 Click **Paste**.

Note

Be sure not to cut anything else before you paste. If you cut or copy other text, the new text replaces the original text in the Clipboard.

Note

You can copy and paste data between documents and between different programs. See *Using Windows 3.1*, Special Edition.

Delete text

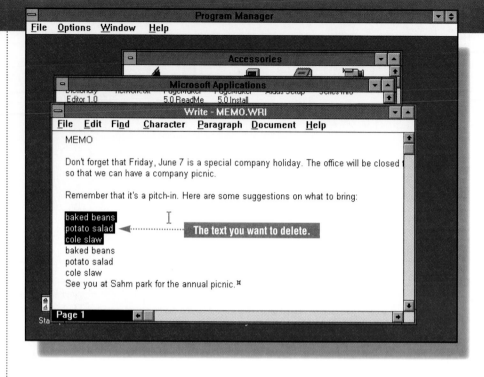

Program Manager

File   Options   Window   Help

Accessories

Microsoft Applications

Write - MEMO.WRI

File   Edit   Find   Character   Paragraph   Document   Help

MEMO

Don't forget that Friday, June 7 is a special company holiday. The office will be closed
so that we can have a company picnic.

Remember that it's a pitch-in. Here are some suggestions on what to bring:

baked beans
potato salad   **The text you want to delete.**
cole slaw
baked beans
potato salad
cole slaw
See you at Sahm park for the annual picnic.

Page 1

Oops!

Be careful when deleting text. If you accidentally delete text you need, you'll have to retype it. Most word processors offer an Undo feature that undoes some changes, such as deleting text. Write does not.

1 **Open the MEMO document file.**
If the document is already open, you can skip this step. If you have not created this document, open a document that you have created.

2 **Click before the *b* in *baked beans*.**
This step positions the insertion point at the beginning of the text that you want to copy.

3 **Press and hold the mouse button, then drag the mouse until you highlight this line and the next two lines.**
This step highlights the section of text that you want to delete.

4 **Press Delete.**
The text is deleted.

After

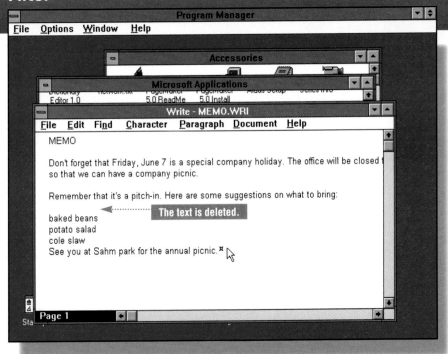

The text is deleted.

1 Select the text that you want to delete.

2 Press **Delete**.

You can also use the Delete and Backspace keys to delete one character at a time. Press Backspace to delete text to the left of the insertion point. Press Delete to delete text to the right of the insertion point.

Center text

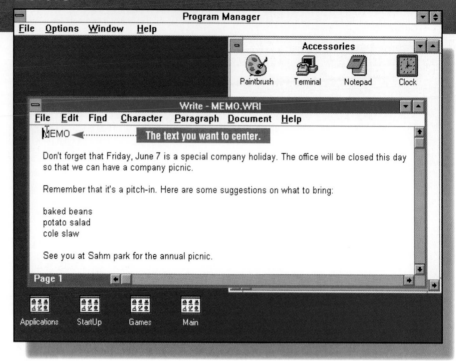

Oops!

Put the insertion point at the beginning of the line and then select the Paragraph Left command to change back to left alignment.

1 **Open the MEMO document file.**
For help with this step, see *TASK: Open a Write document*.

2 **Click before the *M* in *Memo*.**
This step places the insertion point in the line you want to center.

3 **Click Paragraph in the menu bar.**
This step opens the Paragraph menu.

4 **Click Centered.**
This step selects the Centered command. The text is centered on-screen.

5 **Save the document.**
See *TASK: Save a Write document* for help with this step.

After

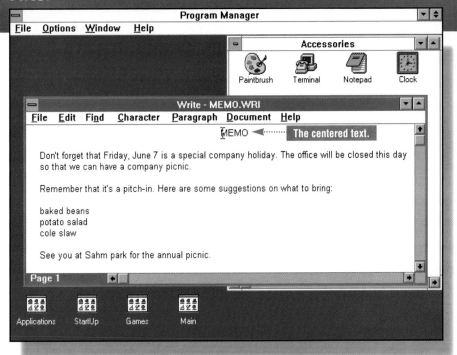

(Program Manager window containing Accessories group with Paintbrush, Terminal, Notepad, Clock icons, and a Write - MEMO.WRI document window)

Write - MEMO.WRI

File Edit Find Character Paragraph Document Help

MEMO ◄········ The centered text.

Don't forget that Friday, June 7 is a special company holiday. The office will be closed this day so that we can have a company picnic.

Remember that it's a pitch-in. Here are some suggestions on what to bring:

baked beans
potato salad
cole slaw

See you at Sahm park for the annual picnic.

Page 1

Applications   StartUp   Games   Main

REVIEW

1 Type the text.

2 Click **Paragraph** in the menu bar.

3 Click the **Centered** command.

Note

You can also choose to justify or right-align the text. Select the option you want from the Paragraph menu.

Make text bold

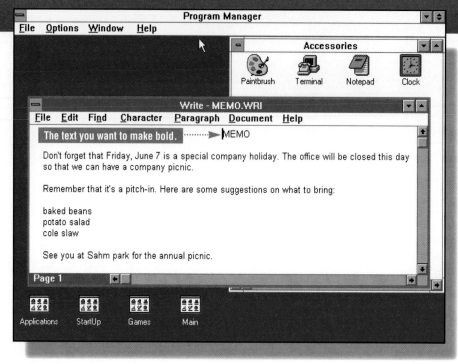

Oops!

To undo the change, select the text and then select the command again.

1 **Open the MEMO document file.**
For help with this step, see *TASK: Open a Write document*. The document appears on-screen. If you do not have a MEMO document, open a document that you do have.

2 **Click before the *M* in MEMO.**
This step places the cursor in the correct position so that you can select the text that you want.

3 **Press and hold the mouse button and drag the mouse until you highlight MEMO.**
This step selects the text that you want to make bold.

4 **Click Character in the menu bar.**
This step opens the Character menu.

5 **Click Bold.**
This step selects the Bold command. The text remains selected on-screen. It appears in boldface. You can follow this same procedure to make other text enhancements, such as italic, underline, and so on. See *Using Windows 3.1*, Special Edition, for more information.

After

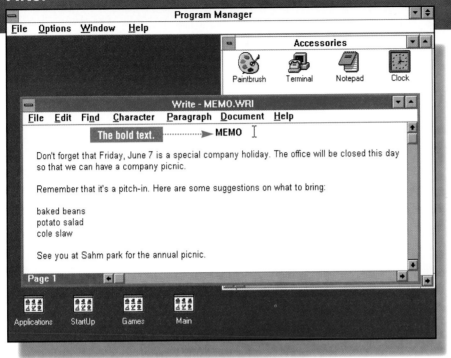

REVIEW

1 Select the text that you want to make bold.

2 Click **Character** in the menu bar.

3 Click **Bold**.

SHORTCUT

Press Ctrl+B to select the Bold command.

Make
text italic

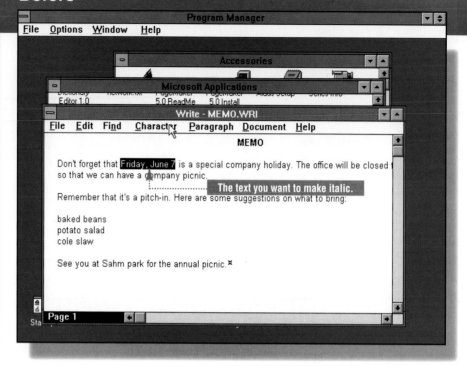

The text you want to make italic.

Oops!

To undo the change, select the text and then select the command again.

1 **Open the MEMO document file.**
For help with this step, see *TASK: Open a Write document*.
The document appears on-screen. If you do not have a
MEMO document, open one that you do have.

2 **Click before the *F* in *Friday*.**
This step places the cursor in the correct position so that you can
select the text that you want.

3 **Press and hold the mouse button and drag the mouse until
you highlight Friday, June 7.**
This step selects the text that you want to make italic.

4 **Click Character in the menu bar.**
This step opens the Character menu.

5 **Click Italic.**
This step selects the Italic command. The text remains selected
on-screen. Click outside the selected text.

After

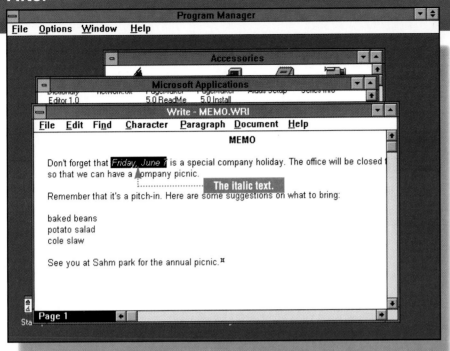

Don't forget that *Friday, June 7* is a special company holiday. The office will be closed so that we can have a company picnic.

The italic text.

Remember that it's a pitch-in. Here are some suggestions on what to bring:

baked beans
potato salad
cole slaw

See you at Sahm park for the annual picnic.

REVIEW

1 Select the text that you want to make italic.

2 Click **Character** in the menu bar.

3 Click **Italic**.

SHORTCUT

Press Ctrl+I to select the Italic command.

Change the font

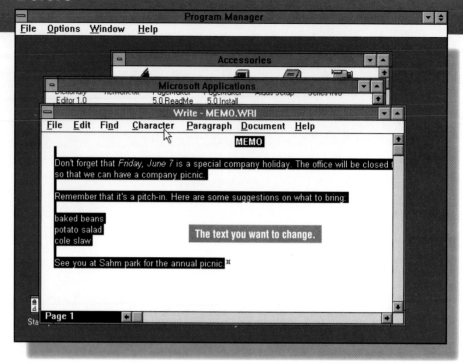

1 **Open the MEMO document file.**
For help with this step, see *TASK: Open a Write document*. The document appears on-screen. If you do not have a MEMO document, open a document that you do have.

2 **Select the entire document.**
To do this, click at the start and drag the mouse across all the text. Then release the mouse button. You can select any amount of text you want.

3 **Click Character in the menu bar.**
This step opens the Character menu.

4 **Click Fonts.**
This step selects the Fonts command. You see the Font dialog box. Depending on what type of printer you have, you may see various fonts listed.

5 **In the Font list, click AvantGarde.**
This step selects the font you want to use. If you don't have this font, select one you do have.

6 **Click OK.**
This step confirms the change. The text is still selected. Click outside the text to deselect it.

After

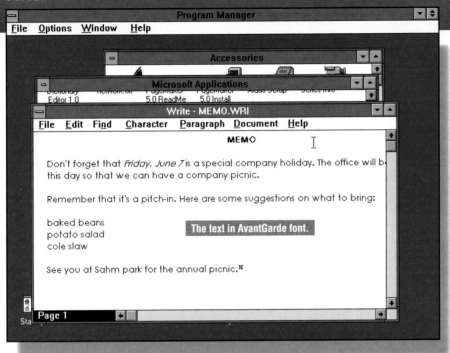

REVIEW

1 Select the text that you want to change.

2 Click **Character** in the menu bar.

3 Click **Fonts**.

4 Click the font you want.

5 Click **OK**.

Note

For more information on fonts, see *Using Windows 3.1*, Special Edition.

Change the font size

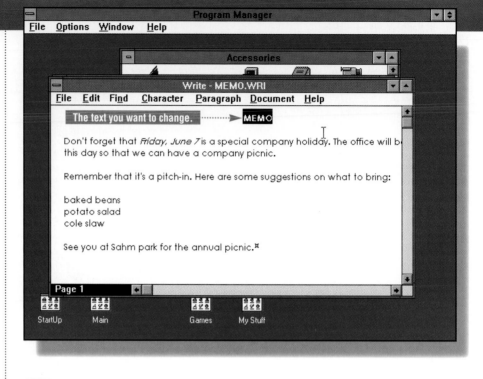

Select the text and then select the Character Reduce Font command to make the text smaller.

1 **Open the MEMO document file.**
For help with this step, see *TASK: Open a Write document.* The document appears on-screen. If you do not have a MEMO document, open a document that you do have.

2 **Click before the *M* in *MEMO*.**
This step places the cursor in the correct position so that you can select the text that you want.

3 **Press and hold the mouse button and drag the mouse until you highlight MEMO.**
This step selects the text that you want to change.

4 **Click Character in the menu bar.**
This step opens the Character menu.

5 **Click Enlarge Font.**
This step selects the Enlarge Font command. The text is still selected. Click outside the text to deselect it.

After

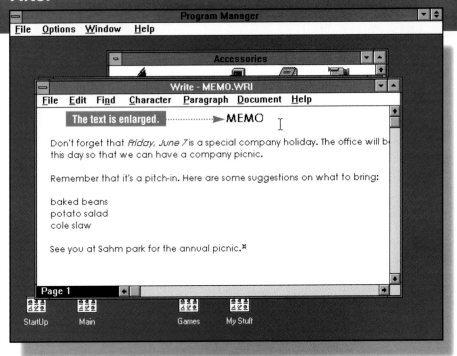

The text is enlarged. ┈┈┈┈┈➤ **MEMO**

Don't forget that *Friday, June 7* is a special company holiday. The office will be this day so that we can have a company picnic.

Remember that it's a pitch-in. Here are some suggestions on what to bring:

baked beans
potato salad
cole slaw

See you at Sahm park for the annual picnic.

REVIEW

1 Select the text that you want to change.

2 Click **Character** in the menu bar.

3 Click **Enlarge Font**.

Indent text

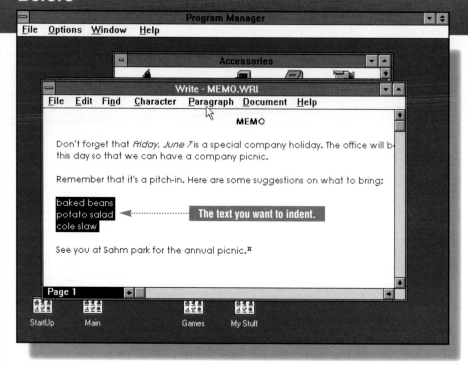

The text you want to indent.

Oops!

Follow these same steps but type 0 for step 5 (task) to unindent the indented text.

1 **Open the MEMO document file.**
For help with this step, see *TASK: Open a Write document*. The document appears on-screen. If you do not have a MEMO document, open a document that you do have.

2 **Select the three lines *baked beans*, *potato salad*, and *cole slaw*.**
These are the lines that you want to indent.

3 **Click Paragraph in the menu bar.**
This step opens the Paragraph menu.

4 **Click Indents.**
This step selects the Indents command. The Indents dialog box appears.

5 **Type .25 in the Left Indent text box**
Typing .25 sets the indent at one-quarter inch.

6 **Click OK.**
This step confirms the new setting. The paragraphs are indented.

After

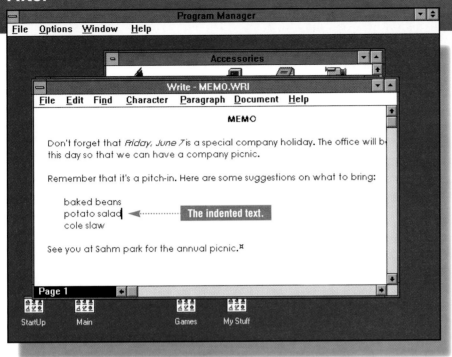

REVIEW

1 Select the text you want to indent.

2 Click **Paragraph** in the menu bar.

3 Click the **Indents** command.

4 Type the values for the indents you want to set: Left Indent, First Line Indent, and Right Indent.

5 Click **OK**.

Note

You can set first-line and right indents by typing the values you want in the Indents dialog box.

Find text

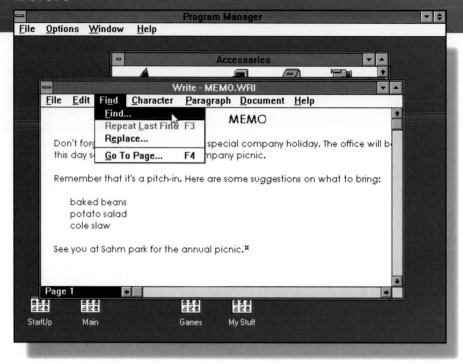

Before

Program Manager

File   Options   Window   Help

Accessories

Write - MEMO.WRI

File   Edit   Find   Character   Paragraph   Document   Help

Find...
Repeat Last Find   F3   MEMO
Replace...
Don't forg   special company holiday. The office will b
this day s   mpany picnic.
Go To Page...   F4

Remember that it's a pitch-in. Here are some suggestions on what to bring:

    baked beans
    potato salad
    cole slaw

See you at Sahm park for the annual picnic.¤

Page 1

StartUp   Main   Games   My Stuff

Oops!

If you see a message
that the text is not
found, click OK. Try
the search again. Be
sure to check your
typing.

1 Open the MEMO document file.
For help with this step, see *TASK: Open a Write document*.
The document appears on-screen. If you do not have a
MEMO document, open a document that you do have.

2 Click Find in the menu bar.
This step opens the Find menu.

3 Click Find.
This step selects the Find command. The Find dialog box appears,
and the cursor is positioned in the Find What text box.

4 Type picnic.
This is the text that you want to find.

5 Click Find Next button
This step starts the search. Write moves to the first occurrence of
the text and selects it. The Find dialog box remains open on-screen.

6 Click Cancel.

After

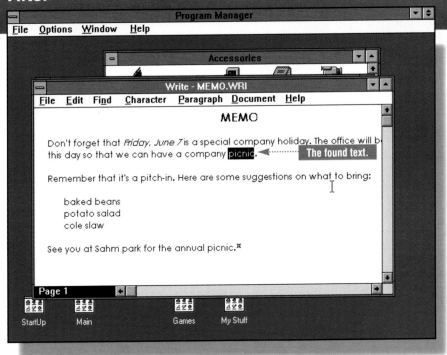

REVIEW

1 Click **Find** in the menu bar.

2 Click the **Find** command.

3 Type the text you want to find.

4 Click the **Find Next** button

5 Double-click the **Control menu box** to close the Find window. Or click **Find Next** to continue the search or click **Cancel** to close the dialog box.

Print a Write document

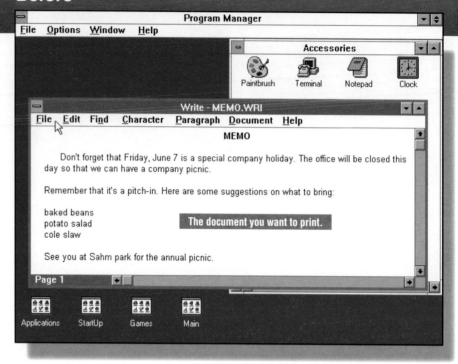

Program Manager

File   Options   Window   Help

Accessories

Paintbrush   Terminal   Notepad   Clock

Write - MEMO.WRI

File   Edit   Find   Character   Paragraph   Document   Help

MEMO

Don't forget that Friday, June 7 is a special company holiday. The office will be closed this day so that we can have a company picnic.

Remember that it's a pitch-in. Here are some suggestions on what to bring:

baked beans
potato salad
cole slaw

The document you want to print.

See you at Sahm park for the annual picnic.

Page 1

Applications   StartUp   Games   Main

Oops!

While the document is printing, you see a dialog box on-screen. Click Cancel to stop printing.

1 **Open the MEMO file.**
For information on this step, see *TASK: Open a Write document.* If you have not created this document, open a document that you have created.

2 **Click File.**
This step opens the File menu. You see a list of File commands.

3 **Click Print.**
This step selects the Print command. The Print dialog box appears on-screen. The insertion point is positioned inside the Copies text box.

4 **Click OK.**
This step tells Write to print one copy of the document.

After

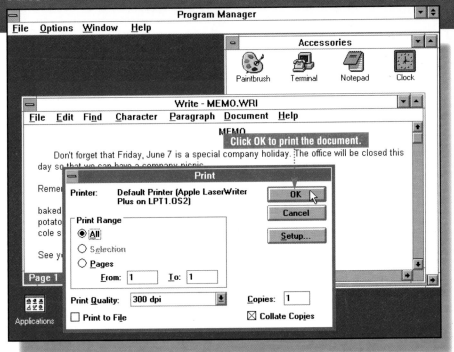

REVIEW

1 Open the file that you want to print.

2 Click **File** to open the File menu.

3 Click **Print** to select the Print command.

4 Click **OK**.

Note

If the document does not print, make sure that you have selected a printer. See *Using Windows 3.1,* Special Edition for more information.

Using Paintbrush

This section covers the following tasks:

- Start Windows Paintbrush

- Draw a circle

- Add text

- Save a Paintbrush drawing

- Open a Paintbrush drawing

- Draw a filled rectangle

- Draw a line

- Erase a drawing

- Add color to an object

Start Windows Paintbrush

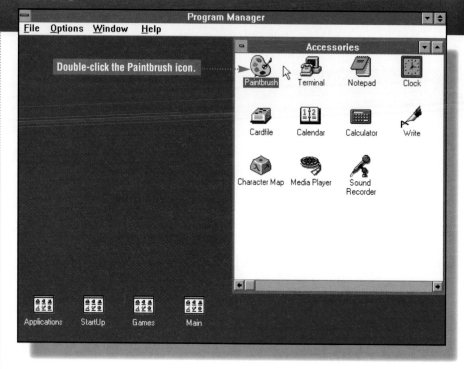

Oops!

To exit Paintbrush, double-click the Control menu box for the Paintbrush window. If you have made any changes, you are prompted to save the drawing.

1 **Double-click the Accessories icon.**

The Paintbrush program is stored in the Accessories program group. To start the program, open the window for that group.

On-screen, you see several icons in a window. The icon for Paintbrush is a palette and brush.

2 **Double-click the Paintbrush icon.**

This step opens the Paintbrush program. You see a blank drawing area on-screen. The title bar reminds you of the name of the program (Paintbrush) and the drawing (Untitled). The drawing remains untitled until you save it.

Along the top of the screen, you see the Paintbrush menu bar. Along the left side of the screen, you see icons for the Paintbrush tools. Along the bottom, you see the color selections.

Notice that Paintbrush offers many paint features. This book covers only basic tasks. Covering all Paintbrush features is beyond the scope of this book. You might want to experiment using what you already know about Microsoft Windows and Microsoft Windows programs. For additional information, see *Using Windows 3.1*, Special Edition.

After

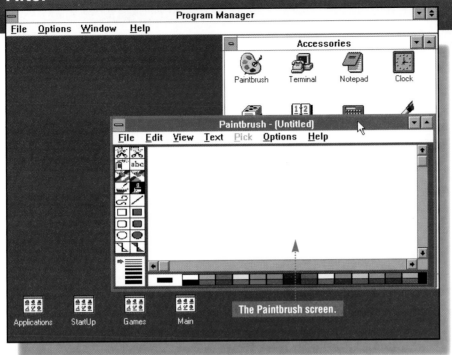

The Paintbrush screen.

REVIEW

1 Double-click the **Accessories** icon.

2 Double-click the **Paintbrush** icon.

Note

If you've been following all the tasks in this section, look in the program group My Stuff. As part of another task, the Paintbrush program was moved to that group.

Draw a circle

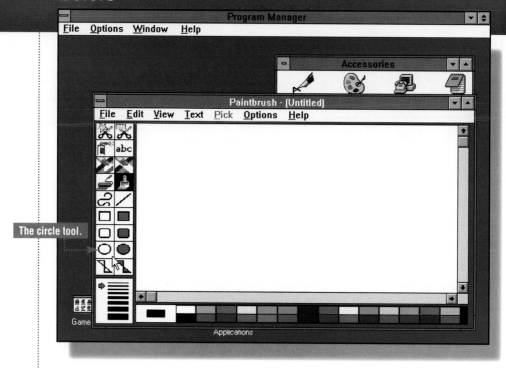

The circle tool.

Oops!

If the circle doesn't appear as you want, click Edit and then Undo to erase the circle.

1 **Start the Paintbrush program.**
For information on this task, see *TASK: Start Windows Paintbrush*. A blank draw area appears on-screen. You might want to resize the window.

2 **Click the circle tool.**
The Paintbrush tools are located along the left side of the window. The circle tool is in the first column near the bottom. Clicking on the tool selects the tool.

3 **Move the mouse pointer into the middle of the draw area.**
When the mouse pointer is on the draw area, it turns into a cross hair.

4 **Press and hold the mouse button and drag the mouse down and to the right until you have created a circle about three inches in diameter. Then release the mouse button.**
Use your best judgment to place and draw the circle. You should see a black circle on-screen.

After

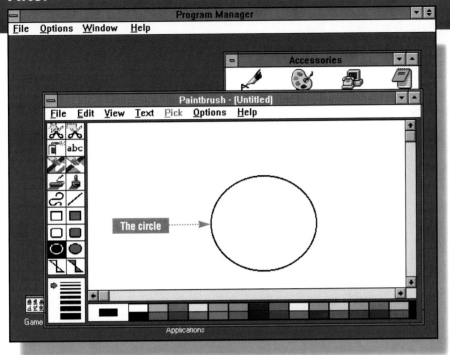

Note

To start over, click File and then New to clear the current drawing. When prompted to save the current image, click No. A blank draw area appears.

REVIEW

Note

To save the drawing, see *TASK: Save a Paintbrush drawing.*

1 Start the **Paintbrush** program.

2 Click the **circle** tool.

3 Press and hold the mouse button and drag the mouse to create a circle.

4 Release the mouse button.

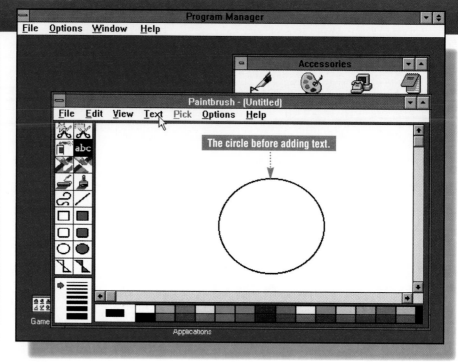

Before

Add text in Paintbrush

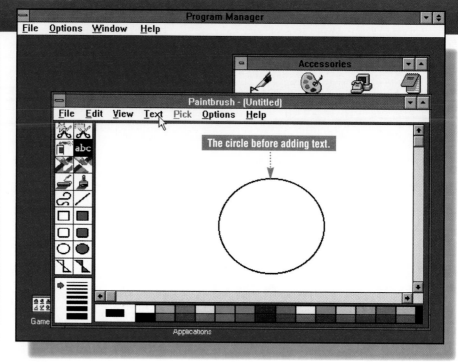

The circle before adding text.

Oops!

Press Backspace to erase the text.

1 **Click the abc tool in the toolbar.**
The abc tool is the text tool and appears in the second column near the top. This tool enables you to insert text.

2 **Click Text in the menu bar.**
This step displays a list of Text commands.

3 **Click Fonts.**
This step displays the Font dialog box.

4 **Type 24 in the Size list box.**
This step selects 24-point type, which is a large type size. If you don't have this size, click one you do have. From the Font dialog box, you can also change the font's style and size.

5 **Click OK.**

6 **Position the mouse pointer just inside the left edge of the circle and click the left mouse button.**
Use your best judgment in placing the mouse pointer. To change the starting point, just click the new spot.

7 **Type Ink, Inc.**
This is the text for the logo. If the text doesn't fit, you can press Backspace to delete it. Then pick a smaller point size. Or start over and draw a bigger circle.

After

REVIEW

1 Click the **abc** tool.

2 Change any font or size settings you want.

3 Click where you want to insert the text.

4 Type the text.

Note

See *TASK: Save a Paintbrush drawing* for help on saving a drawing.

Save a Paintbrush drawing

1 **Click the File menu.**
This step opens the File menu. You see a list of File commands.

2 **Click Save.**
This step selects the Save command and displays the File Save As dialog box. Inside this box, you see a File Name text box. (The mouse pointer is positioned inside this box.) The current directory and a list of directories also are listed.

3 **Type LOGO.**
LOGO is the name that you want to assign to the drawing.

4 **Click OK.**
This step saves the file. The file is saved with the extension BMP. The drawing remains on-screen, and the name appears in the title bar.

After

The file name appears in the title bar.

SHORTCUT

You can also press Ctrl+S to select the File Save command.

REVIEW

1 Click the File Menu

2 Click **Save**.

3 If you have not saved the file already, type a file name.

4 Click **OK**.

Note

After you have saved the file for the first time, simply click File and then Save to save the file again. The file is saved with the same name.

Open a Paintbrush drawing

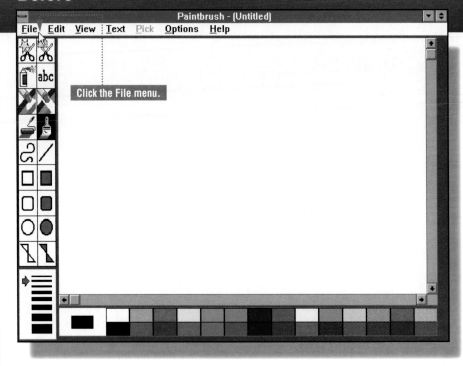

File   Edit   View   Text   Pick   Options   Help

Click the File menu.

Oops!

To close the
Paintbrush program,
save the drawing and
then double-click the
Control menu box for
the Paintbrush
window.

1 **Start the Paintbrush program.**
For information on this task, see *TASK: Start Windows Paintbrush*.
On-screen you see a blank drawing area.

2 **Click the Maximize button.**
The Maximize button is the up arrow in the right corner of the title
bar. This step enlarges the document window so that it fills the
entire screen.

3 **Click File.**
This step opens the File menu. A list of File commands appears.

4 **Click Open.**
This step selects the Open command. The File Open dialog box
appears. This dialog box includes a Filename text box; the cursor is
positioned inside this text box. The current directory is also listed
in the dialog box, and you see two lists: a files list and a directory
list.

5 **Type LOGO.**
LOGO is the name of the file that you want to open. If you do not
have a file named LOGO, select a file that you do have. You can also
point to the file name in the Files list box and click the mouse
button to select the file.

After

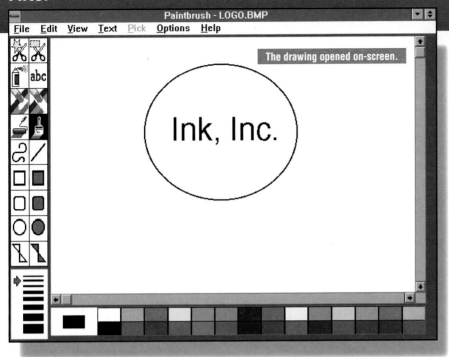

6 **Click OK.**

This step confirms the file name. You see the drawing on-screen. You can make any editing or formatting changes. To save the drawing, click File and then Save.

REVIEW

1 Start the **Paintbrush** program.

2 Click **File** to open the File menu.

3 Click **Open** to select the Open command.

4 Type the name of the file you want to open.

5 Click **OK**.

Note

To see more of the Paintbrush screen, maximize the window. See *TASK: Maximize a window*.

Draw
a filled
rectangle

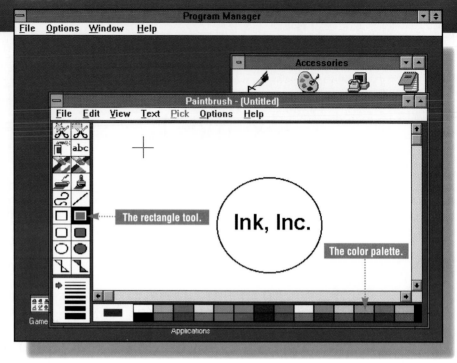

Oops!

If the rectangle
doesn't appear as you
want, click Edit and
then Undo to erase
the rectangle.

1 **Click the filled rectangle tool.**
The Paintbrush tools are located along the left side of the window.
The filled rectangle tool is in the second column near the bottom.
Clicking the tool selects the tool.

2 **Click the Blue color in the color palette.**
This step selects the color you want to use for the fill. Be sure to
click the Blue color in the top row of the color palette.

3 **Move the mouse pointer into the upper left part of the draw
area.**
When the mouse pointer is on the draw area, it turns into a cross
hair.

4 **Press and hold the mouse button and drag the mouse down
and right until you have created a rectangle. Then release the
mouse button.**
You see the rectangle on-screen.

After

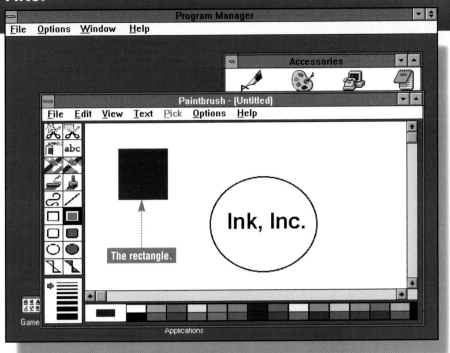

REVIEW

1 Click the **filled rectangle** tool.

2 Select the color you want to use for the fill.

3 Press and hold the mouse button and drag the mouse to create a rectangle.

4 Release the mouse button.

Note

To start over, click File and then New to clear the current drawing. When prompted to save the current image, click No. A blank draw area appears.

Draw a line

Oops!

If the line doesn't appear as you want, click Edit and then Undo to erase the line.

1 **Click the line tool.**
The Paintbrush tools are located along the left side of the window. The line tool is in the second column near the bottom. Clicking on the tool selects the tool.

2 **Click the Red color in the color palette.**
This step selects the color you want to use for the fill. Be sure to click the Red color in the top row of the color palette.

3 **Click the 5th line style.**
The line style palette is next to the color palette. This step selects the width of the line you create.

4 **Move the mouse pointer into the lower left part of the draw area.**
When the mouse pointer is on the draw area, it turns into a cross hair.

5 **Press and hold the mouse button and drag the mouse down and right until you have created a line. Then release the mouse button.**
You see the line on-screen.

After

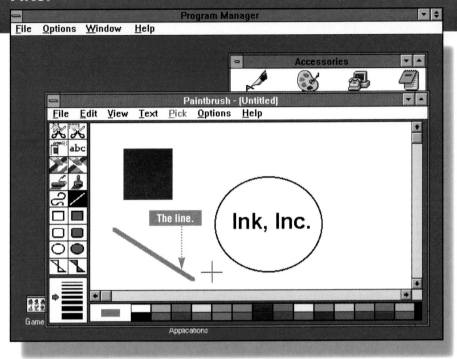

REVIEW

1 Click the **line** tool.

2 Select the color you want to use.

3 Select the line style you want.

4 Press and hold the mouse button and drag the mouse to create a line.

5 Release the mouse button.

Erase a drawing

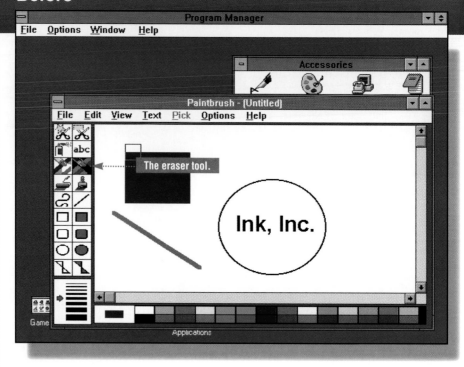

Oops!

Click Edit and then
Undo to undo the
erase.

1 **Click the eraser tool.**
The Paintbrush tools are located along the left side of the window.
The eraser tool is in the second column near the top. Clicking on
the tool selects the tool.

2 **Move the mouse pointer over the rectangle.**
When the mouse pointer is on the draw area, it turns into a blank
rectangle.

3 **Press and hold the mouse button and drag across the
rectangle and line.**
As you drag, the line and rectangle are erased.

After

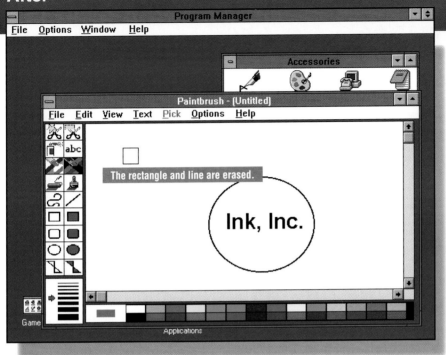

REVIEW

1 Click the **eraser** tool.

2 Press and hold the mouse button and drag across the area you want to erase.

Add color to an object

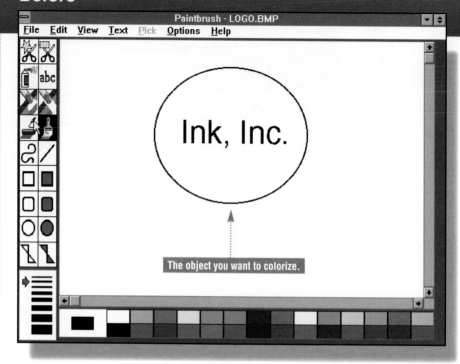

The object you want to colorize.

Oops!

If you don't like the color that you selected, simply follow these same steps and select a different color.

1 **Click the paint roller tool.**
This tool is the fourth one in the first column. This tool fills an item with color.

2 **Click light blue in the color bar along the bottom of the window.**
Light blue is the sixth color in the top row. You can choose whatever color you want from the color bar.

3 **Click in the circle in the drawing.**
This step fills the circle with the selected color.

4 **Click File and then Save.**
This step saves the drawing.

After

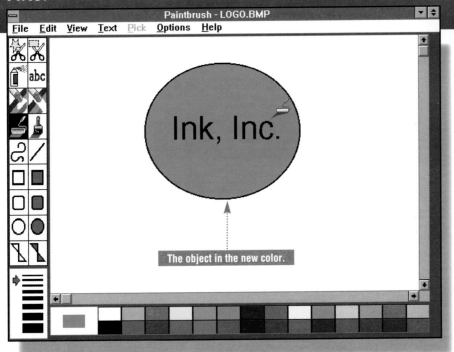

The object in the new color.

REVIEW

1 Click the **paint roller** tool.

2 Click the color you want.

3 Click the item you want to colorize.

Customizing Windows

This section covers the following tasks:

- Change the colors

- Use wallpaper

- Add desktop pattern

- Use the screen saver

Change the colors

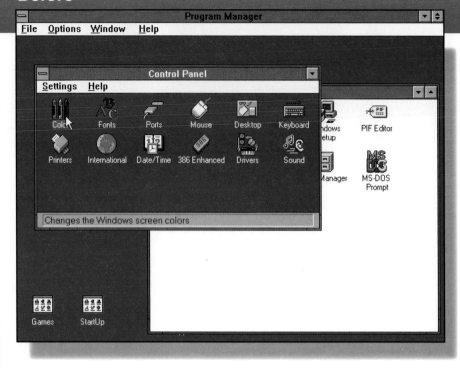

Oops!

Follow this same procedure to change to a different color scheme.

1 Open the Main program group.
To open this program group, double-click the Main icon. The Control Panel is an application stored in this group.

2 Double-click the Control Panel icon.
This step starts the Control Panel. You see icons for several of the Control Panel options. Using the Control Panel, you can add a printer, customize the desktop, change the keyboard, and do other customizing.

3 Double-click the Color icon.
This step opens the Color dialog box. The selected color scheme is listed. (This book uses a custom color scheme. You'll see the color scheme used on your computer.)

4 Click the arrow next to the Color Schemes box.
This step displays a drop-down list of predefined color schemes.

5 Click Valentine.
Click the down scroll arrows to scroll through the list until you find *Valentine*. When you click the scheme, the sample area shows you how the colors will look.

After

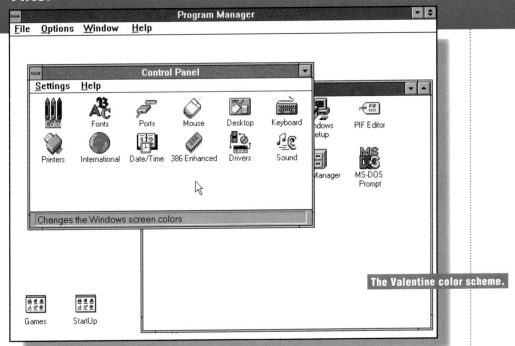

The Valentine color scheme.

6 **Click OK.**

This step confirms the color change. You return to the Program Manager. To close the Control Panel window and the Main window, double-click the Control menu box for each window.

Be sure to click the OK button at the bottom of the Color dialog box not the "fake" one in the sample area.

REVIEW

1 Open the **Main** program group.

2 Double-click the **Control Panel** icon.

3 Double-click the **Color** icon.

4 Click the arrow next to the **Color Schemes** box.

5 Click the color scheme you want.

6 Click **OK**.

Note

To create a custom color scheme, see *Using Windows 3.1*, Special Edition.

Use wallpaper

Oops!

When the Program Manager is maximized, you won't see the wallpaper. Restore the Program Manager so that you can see the desktop area. If you still don't see the wallpaper, open the Desktop dialog box and be sure that Tile is selected in the Wallpaper area.

1 Open the Main program group.
To open this program group, double-click the Main icon. The Control Panel is an application stored in this group.

2 Double-click the Control Panel icon.
This step starts the Control Panel. You see icons for several of the Control Panel options. Using the Control Panel, you can add a printer, customize the desktop, change the keyboard, and do other customizing.

3 Double-click the Desktop icon.
This step opens the Desktop dialog box. You see options that enable you to customize the desktop.

4 Click the arrow next to the File box in the Wallpaper area of the dialog box.
This step displays a drop-down list of predefined wallpaper patterns.

5 Click TARTAN.BMP.
Click the down scroll arrows to scroll through the list until you find this one.

6 Click OK.
This step confirms the change. You are returned to the Program Manager. To close the Control Panel window and the Main window, double-click the Control menu box for each window...

After

The TARTAN wallpaper.

REVIEW

1 Open the **Main** program group.

2 Double-click the **Control Panel** icon.

3 Double-click the **Desktop** icon.

4 Click the arrow next to the **File** box in the Wallpaper area of the dialog box.

5 Click the wallpaper you want.

6 Click **OK**.

Note

You can select any BMP file you want for the wallpaper. You can use Paintbrush to create your own BMP file and then use that as wallpaper.

Add a desktop pattern

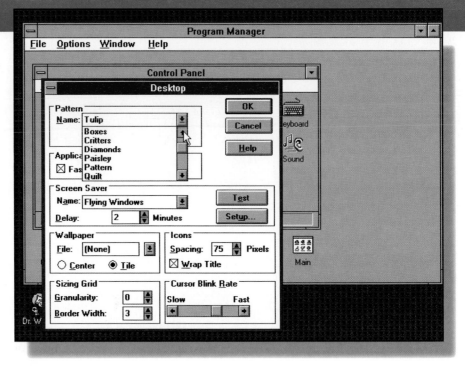

Oops!

When the Program Manager is maximized, you won't see the pattern. Restore the Program Manager so that you can see the desktop area.

1 **Open the Main program group.**
To open this program group, double-click the Main icon. The Control Panel is an application stored in this group.

2 **Double-click the Control Panel icon.**
This step starts the Control Panel. You see icons for several of the Control Panel options. Using the Control Panel, you can add a printer, customize the desktop, change the keyboard, and do other customizing.

3 **Double-click the Desktop icon.**
This step opens the Desktop dialog box. You see options that enable you to customize the desktop.

4 **Click the arrow next to the Name box in the Pattern area of the dialog box.**
This step displays a drop-down list of predefined patterns.

5 **Click Tulip.**
Click the down scroll arrows to scroll through the list until you find this one.

6 **Click OK.**
This step confirms the change. You are returned to the Program Manager. To close the Control Panel window and the Main window, double-click the Control menu box for each window.

After

REVIEW

1 Open the **Main** program group.

2 Double-click the **Control Panel** icon.

3 Double-click the **Desktop** icon.

4 Click the arrow next to the **Name** box in the Pattern area.

5 Click the pattern you want.

6 Click **OK**.

If you've created a custom color scheme, the pattern option might not work. Select one of Windows predefined color schemes and then try the pattern. You also can't choose both wallpaper and patterns. If you select them both, the wallpaper appears rather than the pattern.

Add a desktop pattern

Use the screen saver

Select the screen saver from this list.

Oops!

To stop the screen saver, just press any key or move your mouse.

1 **Open the Main program group.**
To open this program group, double-click the Main icon. The Control Panel is an application stored in this group.

2 **Double-click the Control Panel icon.**
This step starts the Control Panel. You see icons for several of the Control Panel options. Using the Control Panel, you can add a printer, customize the desktop, change the keyboard, and do other customizing.

3 **Double-click the Desktop icon.**
This step opens the Desktop dialog box. You see options that enable you to customize the desktop.

4 **Click the arrow next to the Name box in the Screen Saver area of the dialog box.**
This step displays a drop-down list of screen savers.

5 **Click Flying Windows.**
This step selects the screen saver you want to use. If you want to test the screen saver, click the Test button. Press any key to stop the test.

6 **Click OK.**
This step confirms the change. You are returned to the Program Manager. If you don't use the computer for the preset time (2 minutes), Windows displays the Flying Windows on-screen.

After

The screen saver.

Note

Other companies make screen saver utilities and pictures that you can use. You can display, for example, the deck of the Star Trek Enterprise or flying toasters. AfterDark has the most popular screen saver package.

REVIEW

1 Open the **Main** program group.

2 Double-click the **Control Panel** icon.

3 Double-click the **Desktop** icon.

4 Click the arrow next to the **Name** box in the Screen Saver.

5 Click the screen saver you want.

6 Click **OK**.

Note

You can assign a password to the screen saver so that no one can use your computer. See *Using Windows 3.1*, Special Edition for information on using a password with the screen saver.

Accessory Programs

This section covers the following tasks:

- Use the Calculator
- Display the time
- Use Calendar to add an appointment
- Save a calendar file
- Open a calendar file
- Edit an appointment
- Set an alarm
- Delete an appointment
- Create a note with Notepad

- Open a note
- Edit a note
- Print a note
- Create a cardfile
- Save a cardfile
- Open a card file
- Add cards
- Edit a card
- Find a card
- Print all cards
- Delete a card

Use the Calculator

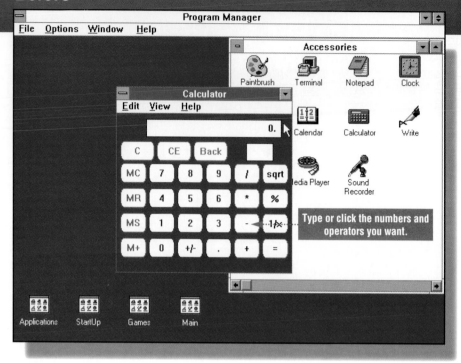

Type or click the numbers and operators you want.

1 Start the Calculator.

The Calculator is stored in the Accessories program group. Open this group window by double-clicking the Accessories group icon. Then double-click the icon for the Calculator. For more information on starting a program, see *TASK: Run a program*.

You see an on-screen version of a calculator. The Calculator has number keys, operator keys (plus, minus, and so on), and other keys. You can enter numbers by typing them from the keyboard or by pointing to them and clicking the mouse button. Use the Calculator as you would a regular calculator.

2 Type 2400.

2400 is the first value that you want to enter. You see this value on the entry line of the Calculator.

3 Type /.

The forward slash (/) is the division key. This tells the calculator that you want to divide 2400 by a number. The entry line still displays 2400.

4 Type 12.

12 is the number by which you want to divide 2400. The equation you have entered is 2400/12, but you see just the number 12 on the entry line.

After

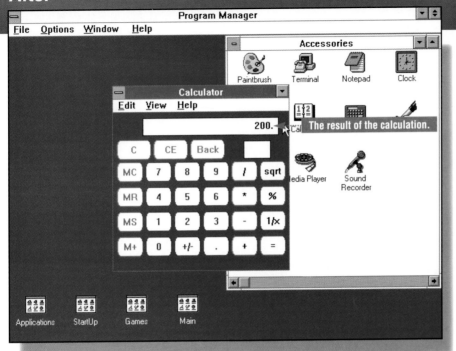

The result of the calculation.

5 **Press Enter.**
Pressing the Enter key tells Microsoft Windows to calculate the formula. You see the result in the entry line (200).

6 **Press Esc.**
Pressing the Esc key clears the entry line so that you can enter another equation.

REVIEW

1 Start the **Calculator**.

2 Type the value that you want to enter. Or click the value in the number pad on-screen.

3 Type or click the mathematical operator that you want (+, –, *, /, and so on).

4 Type the next value.

5 Continue typing values and operators until you complete the equation.

6 Press **Enter**.

Note

If you want to use the numeric keypad to enter numbers, press the Num Lock key. Press the key again to turn off the Number Lock.

Note

You cannot resize the Calculator window.

Display the time

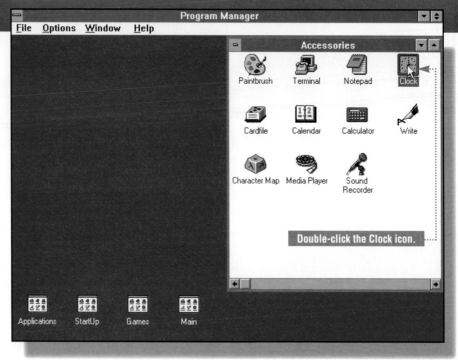

Double-click the Clock icon.

Oops!

To close the clock window, double-click the Control menu box for that window.

1 **Double-click the Accessories group icon.**

This step opens the Accessories group window. You see program icons for all the accessory programs. The clock is stored in this group window.

2 **Double-click the Clock icon.**

This step starts the Clock program. On-screen you see a clock that displays the current time.

After

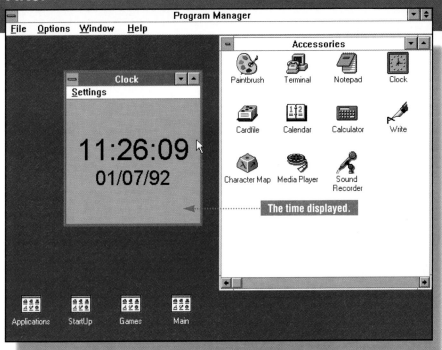

REVIEW

1 Double-click the **Accessories** group icon.

2 Double-click the **Clock** icon.

Note

You can change the clock format from analog (a clock face) to digital (numeric readout). See *Using Windows 3.1*, Special Edition for more information.

Note

If you minimize the clock, the current time is shown on the icon. See *TASK: Minimize a window*.

Use Calendar to add an appointment

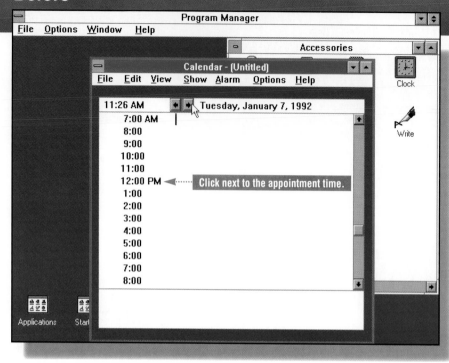

Program Manager
File Options Window Help

Accessories

Calendar - [Untitled]
File Edit View Show Alarm Options Help

11:26 AM ◄ ► Tuesday, January 7, 1992

7:00 AM
8:00
9:00
10:00
11:00
12:00 PM ◄········ Click next to the appointment time.
1:00
2:00
3:00
4:00
5:00
6:00
7:00
8:00

Clock

Write

Applications   Start

Oops!

To delete an appointment, see *TASK: Delete an appointment.*

---

1 Start the Calendar accessory.

You use the Calendar accessory to enter appointments. To start Calendar, double-click the Accessories group icon. Then double-click the Calendar icon. For information on this step, see *TASK: Run a program.*

You see an appointment listing for the current date. The current date and time are displayed at the top of the window under the menu bar. Between the date and time, you also see two scroll arrows. You use these arrows to scroll from date to date. Along the right of the window are two other scroll arrows. You use these arrows to scroll to a different time.

2 Click the right-arrow key that is next to the date.

This step displays the next day's date. (The current date is different from the one that you see in the Before and After screens.)

3 Click 12:00 PM.

This step moves the flashing insertion point to the right of 12:00 PM. You want to enter an appointment for this time.

4 Type Lunch with Alana Moore.

This text describes the appointment you are entering. The text can be up to 80 characters long.

You can continue to add other appointments. After you finish, you must save the calendar file. See *TASK: Save a calendar file.*

After

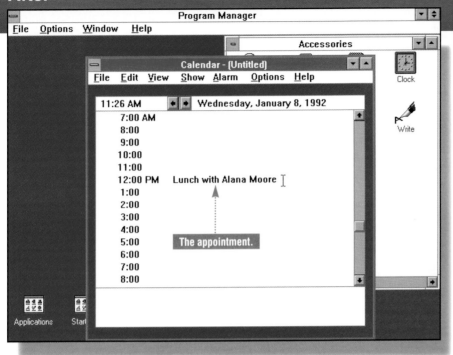

1 Start the **Calendar** accessory.

2 Scroll to the date on which you want to enter an appointment by clicking the scroll arrows at the top of the calendar.

3 Click the time for the appointment.

4 Type the text for the appointment.

5 Save the calendar file.

Note

If you have saved and closed the file and want to add appointments, See *TASK: Open a calendar file.*

Save a calendar file

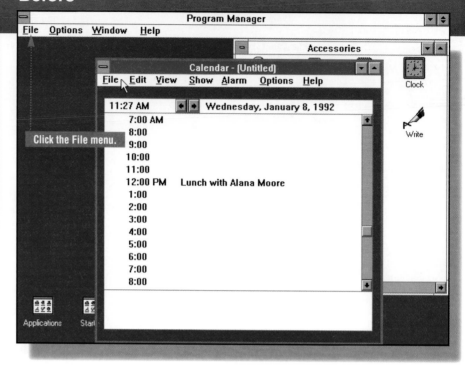

Program Manager

File   Options   Window   Help

Accessories

Clock

Calendar - [Untitled]

File   Edit   View   Show   Alarm   Options   Help

11:27 AM   ◄ ►   Wednesday, January 8, 1992

Click the File menu.

Write

7:00 AM	
8:00	
9:00	
10:00	
11:00	
12:00 PM	Lunch with Alana Moore
1:00	
2:00	
3:00	
4:00	
5:00	
6:00	
7:00	
8:00	

Applications   Start

Oops!

To close the Calendar, save the calendar file and then double-click the Control menu box.

1 **Start the Calendar accessory.**
To start Calendar, double-click the Accessories group icon. Then double-click the Calendar icon. For information on this step, see *TASK: Run a program*.

2 **Enter appointments.**
See *TASK: Add an appointment* for help with this step.

If you have entered appointments already, you can skip steps 1 and 2.

3 **Click File in the menu bar.**
This step opens the File menu. All appointments are saved in a calendar file. You can keep several calendar files. You might have one to keep track of projects and one to keep track of personal appointments, for example.

4 **Click Save.**
This step selects the Save command and displays the File Save As dialog box. Inside this box you see a File Name text box. (The mouse pointer is positioned inside this text box.) The current directory and a list of directories are listed in the dialog box.

5 **Type BUSINESS.**
BUSINESS is the name you want to assign to the calendar file. The name can be up to eight characters long and cannot contain spaces. As a general rule, use only alphanumeric characters.

After

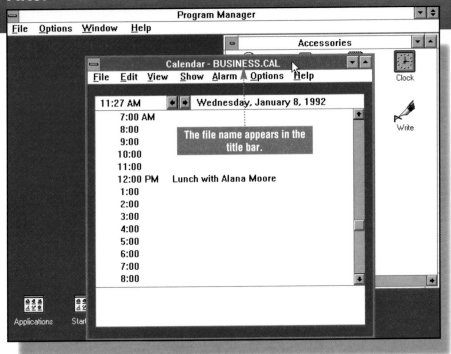

The file name appears in the title bar.

---

6 **Click OK.**

Pressing Enter saves the file. The file is saved with the extension CAL. The calendar file remains on-screen, and the name that you just typed appears in the title bar.

REVIEW

1 Start the **Calendar** accessory.

2 Enter the appointment(s).

3 Click **File** in the menu bar.

4 Click the **Save** command.

5 Type a file name.

6 Click **OK**.

Note

After you have saved the file for the first time, simply click File and then Save to save the file again. The file is saved with the same name.

Open a calendar file

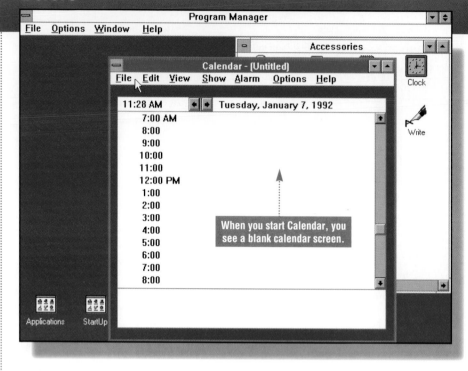

When you start Calendar, you see a blank calendar screen.

Oops!

To close the Calendar, save the calendar file and then double-click the Control menu box for the Calendar window.

1 **Start the Calendar accessory.**
To start Calendar, double-click the Accessories group icon. Then double-click the Calendar icon. For information on this step, see *TASK: Run a program*.

You see a blank appointment listing for the current date. Every time that you start the Calendar accessory, a new, blank calendar file is opened. This file does not contain any entries. To review or edit appointments, open the calendar file first.

2 **Click File in the menu bar.**
This step opens the File menu. You see a list of File commands.

3 **Click Open.**
This step selects the Open command. You see the File Open dialog box. This dialog box includes a File Name text box. (The mouse pointer is positioned inside this text box.) You also see two list boxes: a files list and a directory list.

4 **Type BUSINESS.**
BUSINESS is the name of the file that you want to open. You can also select the file by clicking the file name in the Files list box.

After

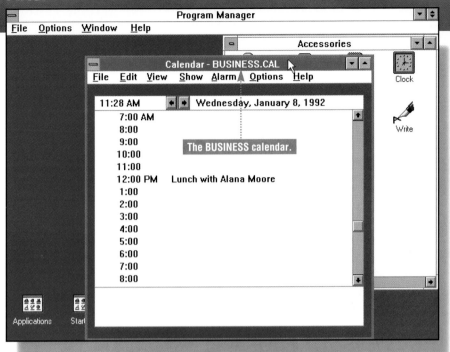

5 **Click** OK.

This step confirms the file name and opens the calendar file. The appointment listings for the current date appear on-screen. If no appointments appear, you didn't schedule any for that day.

REVIEW

1 Start the **Calendar** accessory.

2 Click **File** in the menu bar.

3 Click the **Open** command.

4 Type the name of the file that you want to open.

5 Press **Enter**.

Note

To scroll to other dates, click the scroll arrows below the menu bar.

SHORTCUT

You can also open a file by pointing to the file name with the mouse pointer and then double-clicking the mouse button.

Edit an appointment

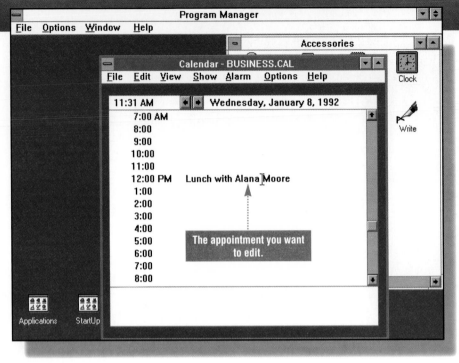

Program Manager

File Options Window Help

Accessories

Calendar - BUSINESS.CAL

File Edit View Show Alarm Options Help

11:31 AM ◄ ► Wednesday, January 8, 1992

7:00 AM
8:00
9:00
10:00
11:00
12:00 PM   Lunch with Alana]Moore
1:00
2:00
3:00
4:00
5:00   The appointment you want
6:00   to edit.
7:00
8:00

Clock

Write

Applications   StartUp

Oops!

To close the Calendar, save the calendar file and then double-click the Control menu box.

1 Start the Calendar accessory.
To start Calendar, open the Accessories program group by double-clicking on the group icon. Then start the program by double-clicking the Calendar icon. For information on this step, See *TASK: Run a program*.

2 Open the BUSINESS file.
See *TASK: Open a calendar file* for help with this step. If you do not have a file named BUSINESS, open a file that you do have.

3 Use the scroll arrows to find the date with the appointment for lunch with Alana Moore.
If you don't have this appointment, scroll to any existing appointment.

4 Click before the *M* in *Moore*.
The insertion point is now positioned to enter the new text.

5 Type and Stephanie.
The previous text scrolls off-screen. This text is still part of the appointment entry; although you don't see the entire entry. The appointment entry is now complete.

6 Press the space bar.
Pressing the space bar inserts a space between the new and existing text.

After

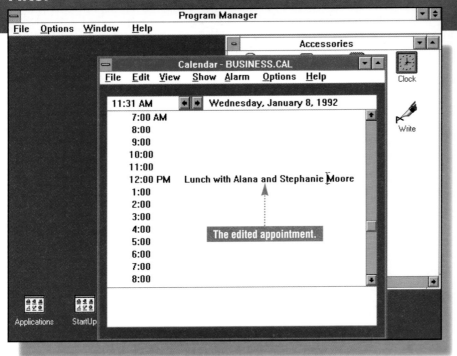

The edited appointment.

7 **Click File and then Save.**
This step opens the File menu and selects the Save command. The edited version of the file is saved to disk, and the file remains on-screen. (See *TASK: Save a calendar file* for more information on this step.)

REVIEW

1 Start the **Calendar** accessory.

2 Open the calendar file that contains the appointment you want to edit.

3 Use the scroll arrows near the top of the window to move to the date of the appointment.

4 Click next to the appointment that you want to edit.

5 Make any changes.

6 Click **File** and then **Save** to save the calendar file.

Note

Every time you start the Calendar, a blank calendar file is opened. To find your appointments, you must open the appropriate calendar file.

Set an alarm

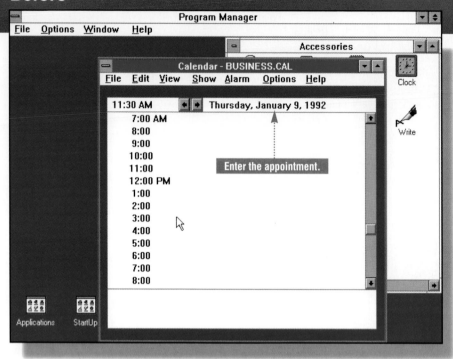

Program Manager

File   Options   Window   Help

Accessories

Calendar - BUSINESS.CAL

File   Edit   View   Show   Alarm   Options   Help

Clock

Write

11:30 AM   Thursday, January 9, 1992

7:00 AM
8:00
9:00
10:00
11:00   Enter the appointment.
12:00 PM
1:00
2:00
3:00
4:00
5:00
6:00
7:00
8:00

Applications   StartUp

Oops!

To turn off the alarm, click the appointment time and select Alarm Set.

1 **Start the Calendar accessory.**
To start Calendar, double-click the Accessories program group icon. Then double-click the Calendar icon. For information on this step, see *TASK: Run a program*.

2 **Open the BUSINESS calendar file.**
See *TASK: Open a calendar file* for help with this step. If you do not have a calendar file called BUSINESS, open a calendar file that you do have. You see the appointment listing for the current date.

3 **Click the scroll arrows until you move to a Thursday date.**
The date for the Thursday differs, depending on the current date (the date on which you start).

4 **Click 3:00 PM.**
You can set an alarm on an appointment that you have entered already or on a new appointment. You will enter a new appointment.

5 **Type Board Meeting.**
Board Meeting describes the appointment.

6 **Click Alarm in the menu bar.**
This step opens the Alarm menu.

After

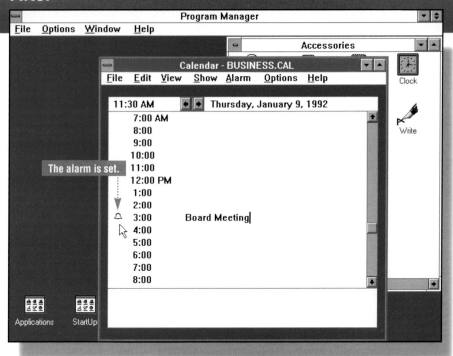

The alarm is set.

SHORTCUT
You also can set an alarm by moving the mouse pointer to the appointment for which you want to set an alarm and pressing the F5 key.

7 **Click Set.**
This step selects the Set command. Next to the appointment time, you see a bell.

8 **Click File and then Save.**
This step opens the File menu, selects the Save command, and saves the calendar file. See *TASK: Save a calendar file* for more information on this step. If Calendar is running, you hear a beep at the appointment time. If the window is open, a dialog box appears that reminds you of the appointment. Click OK to close the dialog box.

Note
For the alarm to sound, you must have the Calendar accessory running with either the window open or the program minimized to an icon.

REVIEW

Note
You can add an alarm to an existing appointment by displaying that appointment, clicking it, and selecting Alarm Set. See *TASK: Edit an appointment*.

1 Start the **Calendar** accessory.

2 Enter a new appointment or display an existing appointment.

3 Click the appointment.

4 Click **Alarm**.

5 Click **Set**.

6 Click **File** and then **Save** to save the calendar file.

Delete an appointment

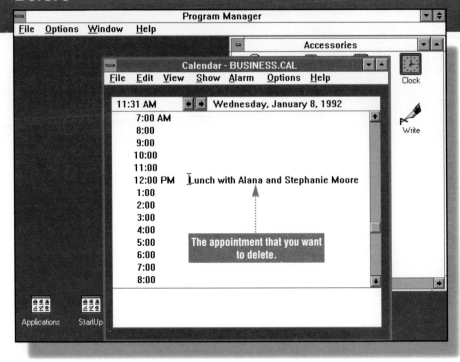

Program Manager

File Options Window Help

Accessories

Calendar - BUSINESS.CAL

File Edit View Show Alarm Options Help

11:31 AM Wednesday, January 8, 1992

7:00 AM
8:00
9:00
10:00
11:00
12:00 PM   Lunch with Alana and Stephanie Moore
1:00
2:00
3:00
4:00
5:00   The appointment that you want
6:00   to delete.
7:00
8:00

Clock

Write

Applications   StartUp

Oops!

If you see a blank calendar when you start, don't worry. Your appointments are not missing. To find them, you must open the calendar file.

1 **Start the Calendar accessory.**
To start Calendar, double-click the Accessories program group icon. Then double-click the Calendar icon. For information on this step, see *TASK: Run a program*.

2 **Open the BUSINESS calendar file.**
If you don't have a calendar file named BUSINESS, open one that you do have. See *TASK: Open a calendar file* for help with this step.

3 **Use the scroll arrows near the top of the window to find the date with the appointment for lunch with Alana and Stephanie Moore.**
If you do not have this appointment, find one that you do have.

4 **Point to the *L* in *Lunch*.**
This step positions the mouse pointer at the beginning of the text that you want to delete. To delete an appointment, you delete the entire text.

5 **Press and hold the mouse button, and then drag the mouse across all of the text.**
This step selects the text for the appointment.

6 **Press the Delete key.**
Pressing the Delete key deletes the selected text.

After

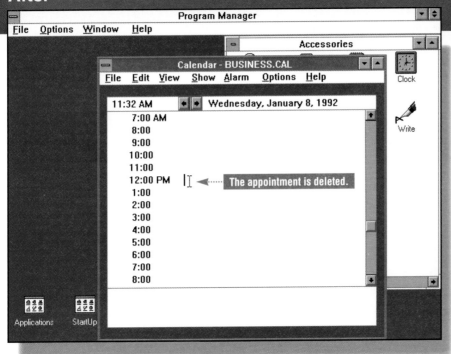

7 **Click File and then Save.**

This step opens the File menu, selects the Save command, and saves the calendar file. See *TASK: Save a calendar file* for more information.

Note

To close the calendar, save the calendar file and then double-click the Control menu box.

REVIEW

Note

You can remove all appointments within a certain date range. See *Using Windows 3.1,* Special Edition for more information.

1 Start the **Calendar** accessory.

2 Open the calendar file that contains the appointment you want to delete.

3 Use the scroll arrows near the top of the window to move to the date of the appointment.

4 Select the appointment text that you want to delete.

5 Delete the appointment text.

6 Click **File** and then **Save** to save the calendar file.

Before

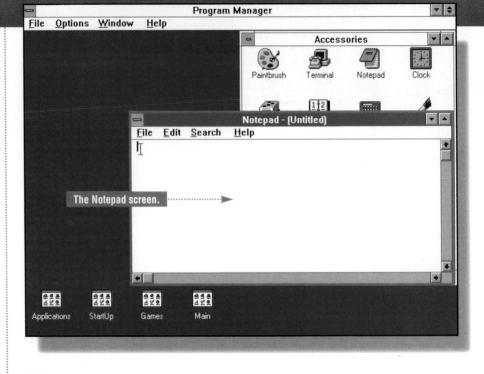

The Notepad screen.

Create a note with Notepad

Oops!

You cannot delete a notepad file through the Notepad accessory. To do so, you must use the File Manager. See *TASK: Delete a file*. To close Notepad, double-click the Control menu box for this window.

1 **Start the Notepad accessory.**
You use the Notepad accessory to enter notes. This program is stored in the Accessories group window. To start Notepad, double-click the Accessories group icon. Then double-click the Notepad icon. (This icon looks like a notepad.)

You see a blank window. The title bar displays Notepad, followed by Untitled. Below the title bar you see the menu bar for Notepad.

2 **Type TO DO LIST.**
TO DO LIST is the note's title, and it reminds you of the note's contents.

3 **Press Enter twice.**
Pressing Enter twice ends the current line, inserts a blank line, and moves the mouse pointer to the next line.

4 **Type Get results from sales survey.**
This is the text of the note. You can enter up to 50,000 characters in a note. You shouldn't have to worry about hitting this limit!

5 **Click File in the menu bar.**
This step opens the File menu. You see a list of File commands.

6 **Click Save.**
This step selects the Save command and displays the File Save As dialog box. Inside this box, you see a Filename text box. (The

After

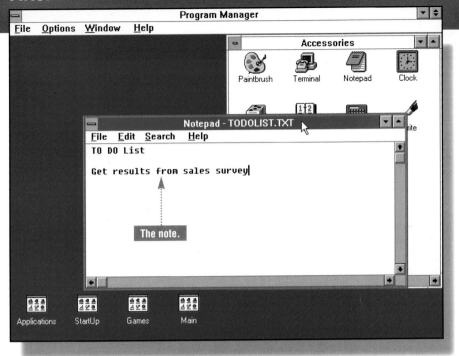

insertion point is positioned inside this box.) The current directory and a list of directories also are listed in the dialog box.

7 **Type TODOLIST.**
TODOLIST is the name of the notepad file. The file is saved automatically with a TXT (indicating text) extension.

8 **Press Enter.**
Pressing Enter confirms the name and saves the file. You still see the note on-screen. The name of the note appears in the title bar.

REVIEW

1 Start the **Notepad** accessory.

2 Type the text for the note.

3 Click the **File** menu.

4 Click **Save**.

5 Type a file name.

6 Press **Enter**.

Note

After you have saved a file for the first time, simply click File and then select Save to save the file again. The file is saved with the same name.

Open a note

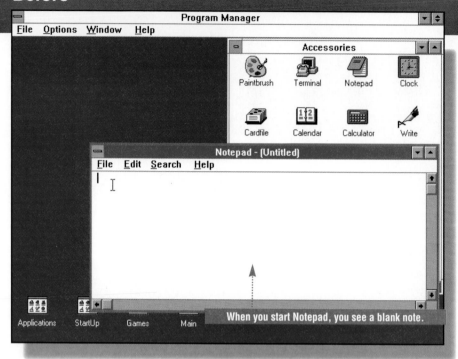

When you start Notepad, you see a blank note.

1 **Start the Notepad accessory.**
To start Notepad, double-click the Accessories group icon. Then double-click the Notepad icon. For information on this step, see *TASK: Run a program*.

On-screen you see a blank note window.

2 **Click File in the menu bar.**
This step opens the File menu. You see a list of File commands.

3 **Click Open.**
This step selects the Open command. You see the File Open dialog box. This dialog box includes a Filename text box. (The mouse pointer is positioned inside this box.) The current directory is also listed in the dialog box, and you see a Files list and a Directory list.

4 **Type TODOLIST.**
TODOLIST is the name of the file that you want to open. You also can select the file by pointing to it in the Files list box and clicking the mouse button.

5 **Press Enter.**
Pressing Enter confirms the file name; the note appears on-screen.

After

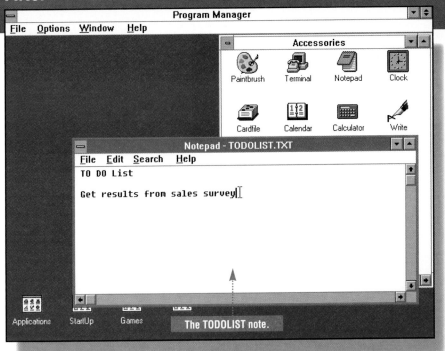

The TODOLIST note.

SHORTCUT

You also can select and open a file by double-clicking the file name in the Files list.

REVIEW

1 Start the **Notepad** accessory.

2 Click **File** in the menu bar.

3 Click the **Open** command.

4 Type the name of the file that you want to open.

5 Press **Enter**.

Note

To close Notepad, save the note and then double-click the Control menu box for that window.

Edit a note

Program Manager

File Options Window Help

Accessories

Paintbrush Terminal Notepad Clock

Cardfile Calendar Calculator Write

Notepad - TODOLIST.TXT

File Edit Search Help

TO DO List

Get results from sales survey

Applications StartUp Games Main

The note you want to edit.

Oops!

If you change your mind about the editing changes, don't save the note.

1 **Start the Notepad accessory**
To start Notepad, double-click the Accessories group icon. Then double-click the Notepad icon. For information on this step, see *TASK: Run a program*.

2 **Open the TODOLIST note.**
If you don't have a note named TODOLIST, open a note that you do have. See *TASK: Open a note* for more information on this step.

3 **Click after the *y* in *survey*.**
The *y* marks the end of the current note, and you want to begin editing here.

4 **Press Enter.**
Pressing Enter ends the line and moves the mouse pointer to the next line.

5 **Type Finish marketing report.**
Typing this text adds to the current note.

6 **Click File and then Save.**
This step opens the File menu and selects the Save command. The new note is saved to disk and replaces the previous version of the note.

After

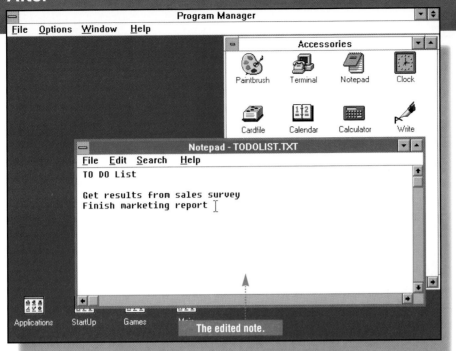

The edited note.

REVIEW

1 Start the **Notepad** accessory.

2 Open the note that you want to edit.

3 Make any editing changes.

4 Click **File** and then **Save** to save the note.

Note

Remember that the Notepad always opens with a new, blank window. From this screen, you open the note that you want.

Print a note

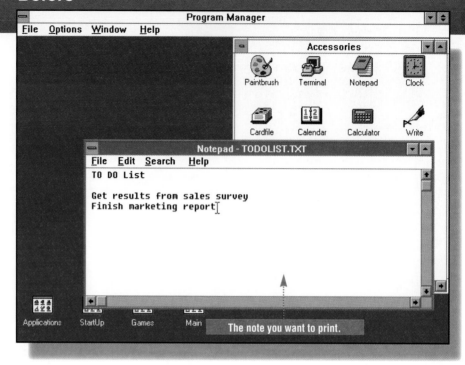

The note you want to print.

Oops!

While the document is printing, you see a dialog box on-screen. Click Cancel to stop printing.

1 **Start the Notepad accessory.**
To start Notepad, double-click the Accessories group icon. Then double-click the Notepad icon. For information on this step, see *TASK: Run a program*.

2 **Open the TODOLIST file.**
TODOLIST is the file that you want to print. If you do not have a file named TODOLIST, open a file that you do have. See *TASK: Open a note* for more information on this step.

3 **Click File in the menu bar.**
This step opens the File menu. You see a list of File commands.

4 **Click Print.**
This step selects the Print command. The note is sent to the printer, which then prints you a paper copy.

After

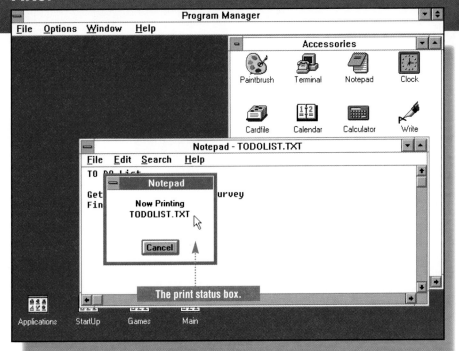

The print status box.

Note

If the note does not print, check to be sure that you have selected a printer. For more information on printer setup, see *Using Windows 3.1*, Special Edition.

Note

To close Notepad, save the note and then double-click the Control menu box for the Notepad window.

REVIEW

1 Start the **Notepad** accessory.

2 Open the note that you want to print.

3 Click **File** in the menu bar.

4 Click the **Print** command.

Create a cardfile

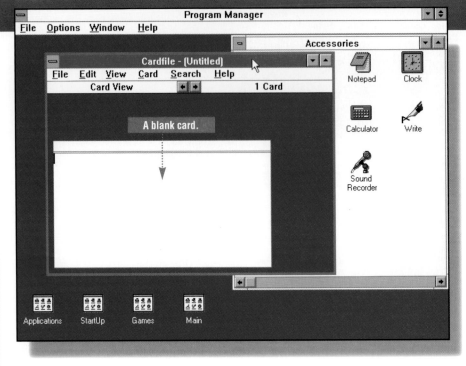

Oops!

To delete a card, see
TASK: Delete a card.

1 **Start the Cardfile accessory.**
To open the Cardfile group window, double-click the Accessories icon. Then double-click the Cardfile icon. (This icon looks like a Rolodex.)

You see a blank card on-screen. The names of the accessory (Cardfile) and (Untitled) appear in the title bar. Below the title bar you see the available menu options.

2 **Type McDaniel, Millie.**
McDaniel, Millie is the text for the first line of the card.

3 **Press Enter.**
Pressing Enter ends the line and moves the mouse pointer to the next line.

4 **Type 5660 South Main Street.**
This text is the address line. You can add more lines to the card.

A card consists of two parts: the text and the index line. Microsoft Windows uses the index line to sort the card. For the first card that you create, you add the text and then the index line. For other cards, you add the index line first. (See *TASK: Add cards.*)

5 **Click Edit in the menu bar.**
This step opens the Edit menu. You see a list of Edit commands.

After

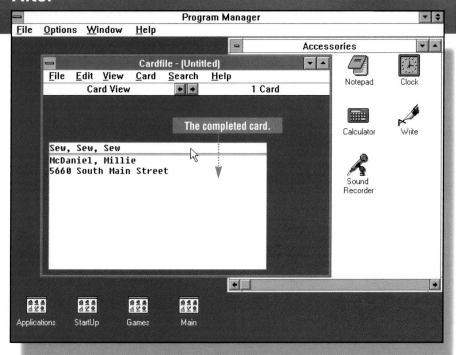

6 **Click Index.**
This step selects the Index command and displays the Index Line dialog box.

7 **Type Sew, Sew, Sew.**
This text is the name of the company and the line that Microsoft Windows uses to sort the entry. It is called the *index line*.

8 **Click OK.**
This step completes entering the index line.

REVIEW

1 Start the **Cardfile** accessory.

2 Type the text of the card.

3 Click **Edit** in the menu bar.

4 Click the **Index** command.

5 Type the index line for the card and click **OK**.

Save a cardfile

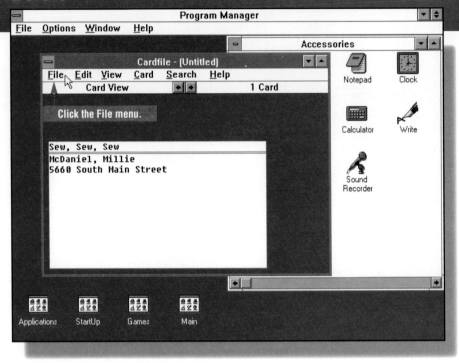

Oops!

Be sure to save the file. If you don't, Microsoft Windows reminds you to save when you close Cardfile.

1 **Start the Cardfile accessory.**
To open the Cardfile accessory, double-click the Accessories icon. Then double-click the Cardfile icon. (This icon looks like a Rolodex.) For information on this step, see *TASK: Run a program*.

2 **Create a cardfile and enter cards.**
See *TASK: Create a cardfile* and *TASK: Add cards* for more information on this step.

3 **Click File in the menu bar.**
This step opens the File menu. You see a list of File commands.

4 **Click Save.**
This step selects the Save command and displays the File Save As dialog box. Inside this box, you see a File Name text box. (The mouse pointer is positioned inside this box.) The current directory and a list of directories are also listed in the dialog box.

5 **Type SHOPS.**
SHOPS is the name that you want to assign to the cardfile. The name can be up to eight characters long and cannot contain any spaces. As a general rule, use only alphanumeric characters.

6 **Click OK.**
This step saves the file. The file is saved with the extension CRD. The card remains on-screen, and the name of the cardfile appears in the title bar.

After

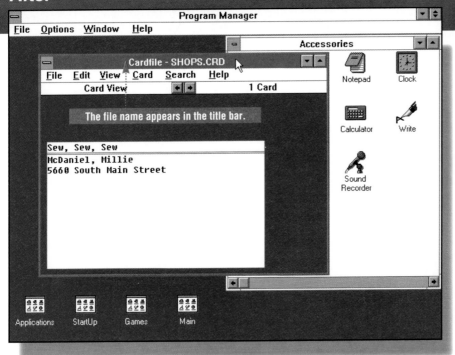

REVIEW

1 Open the **Cardfile** accessory.

2 Create a cardfile and enter the card(s).

3 Click **File** in the menu bar.

4 Click the **Save** command.

5 If you have not saved the file already, type a file name.

6 Click **OK**.

Note

After you have saved a file once, you can click File and then Save to save the file again. The file is saved with the same name.

Open a cardfile

```
Program Manager                                    ▼ ▲
File  Options  Window  Help
                                          Accessories          ▼ ▲
        ▭        Cardfile - [Untitled]          ▼ ▲
          File  Edit  View  Card  Search  Help         Notepad    Clock
          ☟      Card View        ◄ ►        1 Card

                 When you start Cardfile, you see a blank card.      Calculator   Write

                              ▼
                                                      Sound
                                                      recorder


         ◄                                      ►

      Applications   StartUp    Games      Main
```

Oops!

If you see a blank
card when you start,
don't worry. Your
cards are not missing.
To find your cards,
you must open the
cardfile.

1 Start the Cardfile accessory.
To open the Cardfile accessory, double-click the Accessories icon.
Then double-click the Cardfile icon. For information on this step,
See *TASK: Run a program*.

To review, edit, or add cards, you must open the cardfile.

2 Click File in the menu bar.
This step opens the File menu. You see a list of File commands.

3 Click Open.
This step selects the Open command. You see the File Open dialog
box. This dialog box includes a Filename text box. (The mouse
pointer is positioned in this text box.) The current directory is also
listed in the dialog box, and you see a files list and a directory list.

4 Type SHOPS.
SHOPS is the name of the cardfile that you want to open. If you
don't have a file named SHOPS, type the name of one that you do
have. You also can point to the file name in the Files list box and
click the mouse button to select the file.

After

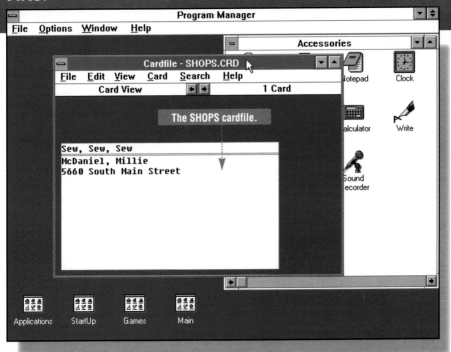

5 Press **Enter**.

Pressing Enter confirms the file name. You see the first card in the cardfile.

As a shortcut, you can double-click the file name in the Files list to select and open the file.

REVIEW

1 Start the **Cardfile** accessory.

2 Click **File** in the menu bar.

3 Click the **Open** command.

4 Type the name of the file that you want to open.

5 Press **Enter**.

Add cards

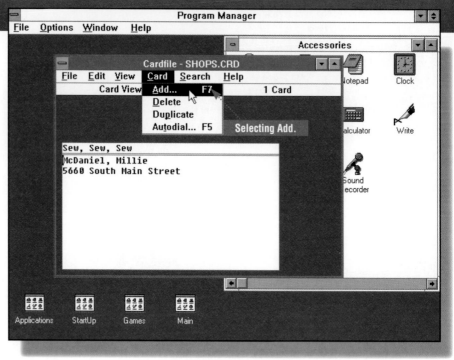

Oops!

When you enter other cards, be sure to open the appropriate cardfile first. Saving the current file over the original file deletes all the cards you have entered previously.

1 **Start the Cardfile accessory.**
To open the Cardfile accessory, double-click the Accessories icon. Then double-click the Cardfile icon.

2 **Open the SHOPS cardfile.**
You see the first card on-screen.

3 **Click Card in the menu.**
This step opens the Card menu.

4 **Click Add.**
This step selects the Add command. The Add dialog box appears on-screen. When you create the first card, you enter the card text and then the index line. With new cards, you must enter the index line first. You enter the index line in the Add dialog box.

5 **Type Country Crafts.**
Country Crafts is the index line for the card. The card is sorted by its index line.

6 **Click OK.**
Pressing Enter confirms the index line and creates a new card.

7 **Type Ball, Darlene and press Enter.**
This text is the name of the shop owner. Notice that the other cards in this cardfile use the same format (last name first). Pressing Enter ends the line and moves the mouse pointer to the next line.

After

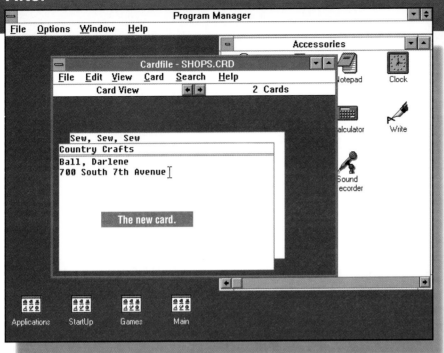

Note

To delete a card, see
TASK: Delete a card.

8 **Type 700 South 7th Avenue.**
This text is the address line.

9 **Click File and then Save.**
This step opens the File menu, selects the Save command, and
saves the file.

Note

Use the same format
for new cards that you
did for the first card
that you created. This
keeps the information
better organized.

REVIEW

1 Open the **Cardfile** accessory.

2 Open the cardfile that you want to use.

3 Click **Card**.

4 Click **Add**.

5 Type the index line for the card.

6 Click **OK**.

7 Type the text of the card.

8 Click **File** and then **Save** to save the cardfile.

Edit a card

Program Manager

File Options Window Help

Accessories

Cardfile - SHOPS.CRD

File Edit View Card Search Help

Card View   2 Cards

Sew, Sew, Sew
Country Crafts
Ball, Darlene
700 South 7th Avenue

Notepad   Clock

alculator   Write

Sound
ecorder

The card you want to edit.

Applications   StartUp   Games   Main

Oops!

If you see a blank card when you start, don't worry. Your cards are not missing. To find your cards, you must open the cardfile.

1 **Start the Cardfile accessory.**
To open the Cardfile accessory, double-click the Accessories icon. Then double-click the Cardfile icon. For information on this step, see *TASK: Run a program*.

2 **Open the SHOPS cardfile.**
SHOPS is the cardfile that contains the card you want to edit. See *TASK: Open cardfile* for more information. You see the Country Crafts card on-screen, which is the first card—alphabetically—of the cards that you have entered.

3 **Press the PgDn key.**
Pressing the PgDn key displays the next card. You want the card titled *Sew, Sew, Sew*.

(If you have not created the cards for other cardfile tasks, you will not find this card. Find one that you do have.)

4 **Click after the *t* in *Street*.**
This step positions the mouse pointer at the location where you want to add new text.

5 **Press Enter.**
Pressing Enter ends the line and moves the mouse pointer to the next line.

After

The edited card.

6 **Type Dolls, jumpers, quilts.**
This new text is added to the card.

7 **Click File and then Save.**
This step opens the File menu, selects the Save command, and
saves the cardfile.

REVIEW

1 Start the **Cardfile** accessory.

2 Open the cardfile that contains the card you want to edit.

3 Use the scroll arrows to move to the card. Or press the **PgDn** or
PgUp key to move to the card.

4 Click next to the line that you want to edit.

5 Make any changes.

6 Click **File** and then **Save** to save the cardfile.

Find a card

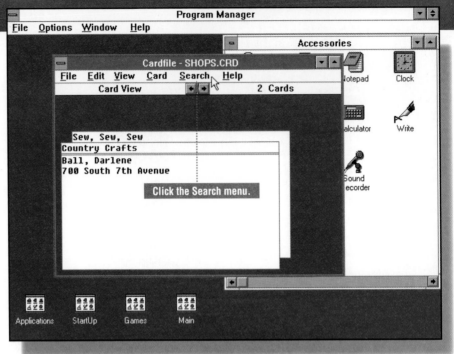

Oops!

If you see a blank card when you start, don't worry. Your cards are not missing. To find your cards, you must open the cardfile.

1 **Start the Cardfile accessory.**
To open the Cardfile accessory, double-click the Accessories icon. Then double-click the Cardfile icon. For information on this step, see *TASK: Run a program*.

2 **Open the SHOPS cardfile.**
The SHOPS cardfile contains the card that you want to find.
See TASK: Open cardfile for more information.

3 **Click Search in the menu bar.**
This step opens the Search menu.

4 **Click Find.**
This step selects the Find command. You see the Find dialog box. (The mouse pointer is positioned inside this text box.)

5 **Type quilts.**
Quilts is the text that you want to find. (Note that if you didn't add this text to the card in *TASK: Edit a card*, you will not be able to find it now. If so, search for text on a card that you do have.)

6 **Click Find Next.**
Pressing Enter starts the search. Microsoft Windows moves to the first card that contains *quilts*. This is the card for Sew, Sew, Sew.

After

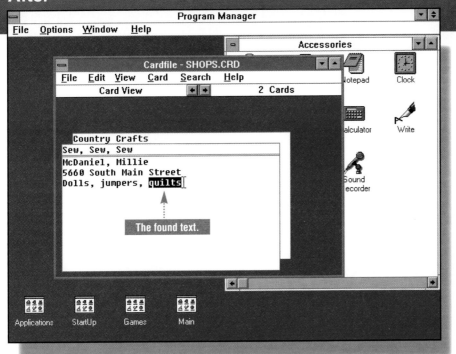

The found text.

SHORTCUT

To find the next match, click Search and then Find Next. Notice that Find does not search the index line.

REVIEW

 Start the **Cardfile** accessory.

2 Open the cardfile that contains the card you want to find.

3 Click **Search** in the menu bar.

4 Click the **Find** command.

5 Type the text for which you want to search.

6 Click **Find Next**.

Note

If no match is found, you see an alert box that says `Cannot find text`. (The word *text* is replaced by the text for which you were searching.)

Print all cards

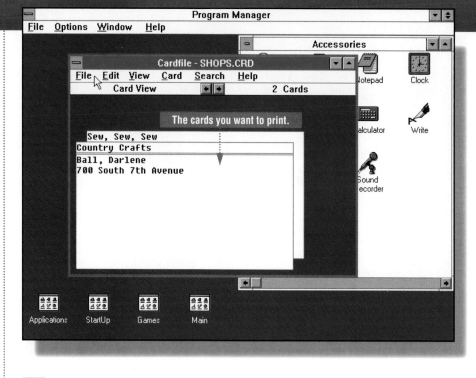

File   Options   Window   Help

Accessories

Cardfile - SHOPS.CRD

File   Edit   View   Card   Search   Help

Card View   2 Cards

The cards you want to print.

Sew, Sew, Sew
Country Crafts
Ball, Darlene
700 South 7th Avenue

Notepad   Clock

alculator   Write

Sound
ecorder

Applications   StartUp   Games   Main

Oops!

While Microsoft
Windows is printing,
you see a dialog box
on-screen that
contains a Cancel
button. Click Cancel
to stop printing.

1 **Start the Cardfile accessory.**
To open the Cardfile group window, double-click the Accessories
icon. Then double-click the Cardfile icon to start the program.
For information on this step, see *TASK: Run a program*.

2 **Open the SHOPS file.**
You will print all the cards in the SHOP file. See *TASK: Open a
cardfile* for more information on this step. If you do not have this
cardfile, open one that you do have.

3 **Click File in the menu bar.**
This step opens the File menu. You see a list of File commands.

4 **Click Print All.**
This step selects the Print All command. All cards are printed.

After

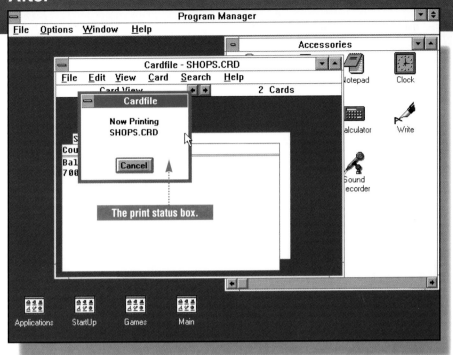

The print status box.

REVIEW

1 Start the **Cardfile** accessory.

2 Open the cardfile that you want to print.

3 Click **File** in the menu bar.

4 Click the **Print All** command.

Note

If the cards do not print, make sure that you have selected a printer. For more information, see *Using Windows 3.1,* Special Edition.

Delete a card

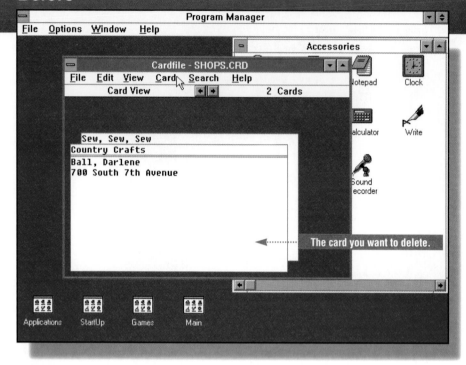

The card you want to delete.

Oops!

If you decide that you do not want to delete the card, click Cancel in step 5.

1 **Start the Cardfile accessory.**
To start the Cardfile accessory, double-click the Accessories icon. Then double-click the Cardfile icon. For information on this step, see *TASK: Run a program*.

2 **Open the SHOPS cardfile.**
The SHOPS cardfile contains the file that you want to delete. See *TASK: Open a cardfile* for more information. If you don't have this cardfile, open one that you do have.

The first card in the stack, Country Crafts, appears. You want to delete this card. If this card doesn't appear, use the scroll arrows below the menu bar to scroll to the card.

3 **Click Card in the menu bar.**
This step opens the Card menu.

4 **Click Delete.**
This step selects the Delete command. You see an alert box that says Delete "Country Crafts"?.

5 **Click OK.**
This step confirms the deletion. The card is deleted.

6 **Click File and then Save.**
This step opens the File menu, selects the Save command, and saves the cardfile.

After

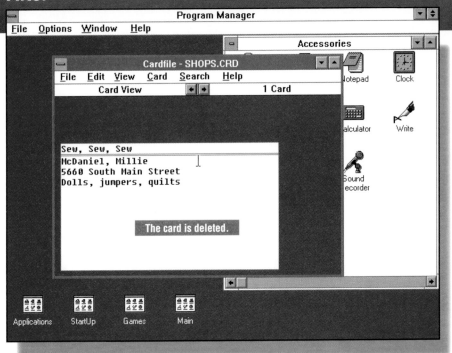

1 Start the **Cardfile** accessory.

2 Open the cardfile that contains the card you want to delete.

3 Use the scroll arrows or the **PgDn** and **PgUp** key to move to the card that you want to delete.

4 Click **Card** in the menu bar.

5 Click the **Delete** command.

6 Click **OK**.

7 Click **File** and then **Save** to save the cardfile.

Note

If you see a blank card when you start, don't worry. Your cards are not missing. To find your cards, you must open the cardfile.

Reference

- Quick Reference

- Guide to Basic Keyboard Operations

- Glossary

Quick Reference

Task	Procedure
Select an icon	Click the icon.
Select a window	Click the window.
Open a window	Double-click the window icon.
Start a program	Double-click the program icon.
Quit a program	Double-click the Control menu box.
Move a window	Click the title bar, press and hold the mouse button, and drag the window to a new location. Release the mouse button.
Resize a window	Position mouse on a border. Press and hold the mouse button, and drag the borders to change the size. Release the mouse button.
Minimize a window	Click the **Minimize** button.
Maximize a window	Click the **Maximize** button.
Help	Click **Help** in the menu bar.
Quit Windows	Double-click the **Control menu box** of the Program Manager.
Select a file (File Manager)	Click the file.
Select a directory (File Manager)	Click the directory.
Select a drive (File Manager)	Click the drive icon.
Collapse the selected directory (File Manager)	Double-click the directory.
Expand the selected directory (File Manager)	Double-click the directory icon.
Create directory (File Manager)	Select **File Create Directory**.
Search for file (File Manager)	Select **File Search**.
Copy file (File Manager)	Select **File Copy** or press the **F8** key.
Delete file (File Manager)	Select **File Delete** or press the **Del** key.
Rename file (File Manager)	Select **File Rename** or press the **F7** key.
Move file (File Manager)	Select File Move.

Guide to Basic Keyboard Operations

Instead of using the mouse with Microsoft Windows, you can use the keyboard. This section covers some basic keyboard operations. For complete instructions on using the keyboard, see *Using Windows 3.1*, Special Edition.

Open a menu

1. Press the **Alt** key to select the menu bar.

2. Use the ← or → key to move to the menu that you want to open.

3. Press **Enter**.

To open a menu quickly, press the **Alt** key and then type the underlined letter in the menu name.

Select a menu command

1. Open the menu.

2. Use the ↑ or ↓ key to move to the command that you want to open.

3. Press **Enter**.

To select a menu command quickly, type the underlined letter in the menu command name.

Select an option in a dialog box

Press and hold the **Alt** key; then type the underlined letter in the check box, text box, or list box.

Open the Control menu for an application window

Press the **Alt** key and then press the **space bar**.

Glossary

application A computer program that is used for a particular task such as word processing. In most cases, *program* and *application* mean the same thing and can be used interchangeably.

check box A square box that appears in a dialog box. Check boxes can be checked (selected) or unchecked (unselected).

click The action of pressing and releasing the mouse button.

Clipboard A temporary spot in memory that holds the text or graphics that you cut or copy.

close To remove a window from the desktop.

command button A choice of action that appears in a dialog box. Two common command buttons are OK and Cancel.

Control menu box The hyphen or little box that appears in the title bar of a window. Clicking on this box opens the Control menu. You use this menu to manipulate the window.

desktop The screen background where windows and icons appear.

dialog box An on-screen window that displays further command options. Often, a dialog box reminds you of the consequences or results of a command and asks you to confirm that you want to proceed with the action.

directory A disk area that stores information about files. A directory is like a drawer in a file cabinet. Within that drawer, you can store several files.

directory tree A graphical display in a window of the directories on disk. The directory tree appears when you use the File Manager.

DOS An acronym for disk operating system. DOS manages the details of your system, such as storing and retrieving programs and files.

double-click The action of pressing the mouse button twice in rapid succession.

drag The mouse movement of pointing to an item and then pressing and holding the left mouse button as you move the mouse.

drop-down list box A box that lists the default choice in a dialog box. Other choices are available. To display the other choices, click the arrow in the square box at the right of the drop-down list box.

file The various individual reports, memos, databases, and letters that you store on your hard drive (or floppy disk) for future use.

file name The name that you assign a file when you store it to disk. A file name consists of two parts: the root and the extension. The root can be as many as eight characters long. The extension can be three characters long, and it usually indicates the file type. The root and extension are separated by a period. SALES.DOC is a valid file name—SALES is the root, and DOC is the extension.

format The initialization process that prepares a disk for use.

graphical user interface (GUI) A visual environment that enables you to learn a computer program more intuitively and to use a computer program more easily.

group A collection of programs. These programs are stored in a group window, which is represented by a group icon.

icon An on-screen picture that represents a group window, an application, a document, or other elements within Microsoft Windows.

list box A box within a dialog box that displays a list of items such as file names.

Maximize button The small up-arrow at the right of the title bar of a window.

menu bar A list of menu names near the top of the window.

Minimize button The small down-arrow at the right of the window's title bar.

mouse pointer The on-screen symbol that moves when you move the mouse. The pointer changes shape depending on what task you are performing, such as typing text, selecting a command, and so on.

open The action of displaying the contents of a window on-screen.

option button A round button that appears in a dialog box. To select an option, click the option button. A dot appears in the button. You cannot activate more than one option button at a time.

path The route, through directories, to a program or document file. The path C:\WINDOWS\TEMP\REPORT.DOC, for example, includes four elements: the disk drive (C:); the first directory (WINDOWS); the subdirectory, which is a directory within the first directory (TEMP); and the file name (REPORT.DOC).

root directory The main directory. The root directory contains all other directories.

scroll bars The bars at the bottom and right of a window. At the ends of the bars are scroll arrows; click an arrow to scroll the window in the direction of the arrow.

text box A box within a dialog box. You type information—such as a file name—into the box to complete the command.

title bar The horizontal bar at the top of a window. The title bar contains the name of the window. Often, the title bar also contains the Control menu box (at the left) and the Maximize and Minimize buttons (at the right).

wild card Characters that stand for any other character that may appear in the same place. In Microsoft Windows, you can use the asterisk (*), which stands for any character (and any number of characters), and the question mark (?), which stands for any one character.

window A rectangular area on-screen in which you view an application or a document. A window can contain icons that represent applications, the application itself, or a document you have created in an application. Everything in Microsoft Windows is contained in a window.

Where To Get More Help

This book does not cover every Microsoft Windows feature or every way to complete a task. This book is for the beginning user. As you become more comfortable, you may need a more complete reference book. Que offers several Microsoft Windows books to suit your needs:

> *Using Windows 3.1*, Special Edition
> *Windows 3.1 QuickStart*
> *Windows 3.1 Quick Reference*

Also of interest:

> *Que's Computer User's Dictionary*, 4th Edition
> *Introduction to Personal Computers*, 4th Edition

And if you have Windows programs, you might want to read the following Que books:

> *Using 1-2-3 Release 4 for Windows*, Special Edition
> *Using Excel Version 5 for Windows*, Special Edition
> *Using Word Version 6 for Windows*, Special Edition
> *Using WordPerfect Version 6 for Windows*, Special Edition

Index